To Hannah,

we all hope you
enjoy this book, and
that it inspires you
to keep writing.

BLOOD, WATER, WIND, AND STONE

editor

D1507742

BLOOD, WATER, WIND, AND STONE

An Anthology of Wyoming Writers

edited by

LORI HOWE

Sastrugi Press

San Diego • Jackson Hole

Sastrugi Press / Published by arrangement with the authors

Blood, Water, Wind, and Stone: An Anthology of Wyoming Writers

FICTION: Works in this section are works of fiction. Names, characters, businesses, places, events and incidents are either the products of the author's imagination or used in a fictitious manner. Any resemblance to actual persons, living or dead, or actual events is purely coincidental.

Sastrugi Press LLC
PO Box 1297, Jackson, WY 83001
www.sastrugipress.com

Library of Congress Catalog-in-Publication Data
Library of Congress Control Number: 2016954656
Edited by Lori Howe
Sastrugi Press — 1st United States edition
p. cm.
1. Anthologies 2. Short Stories 3. Poetry 4. Contemporary fiction
Summary: Blood, Water, Wind, and Stone, an anthology of Wyoming poets and writers, offers the reader a look into the daily mercies and wonder of life lived in a state of such great isolation and beauty.
ISBN-13: 978-1-944986-03-2
ISBN-10: 1-944986-03-0

810.8'

Cover image: Susan Davis

Printed in the United States of America

10 9 8 7 6 5 4 3 2 1

Table of Contents

NONFICTION   79

FICTION

Acknowledgements

It has been my good fortune to serve as editor of this anthology, and I offer my gratitude for the hard work and dedication of writers and writers' groups across Wyoming, as well as to Aaron Linsdau and everyone at Sastrugi Press, without whom this book would have been nothing more than a good idea. Special thanks, too, to Wyoming photographer Susan Davis, whose luminous work graces our cover and embodies the natural beauty of Wyoming. Infinite thanks to the Wyoming Humanities Council and the ThinkWY Roads Scholar program, for generously funding the poetry workshop tour through which I met and wrote with a great many of these magnificent poets and writers. My gratitude, also, to the hardworking staff of libraries around the state who hosted those workshops, and to the merchants who have offered to host readings and signings for *Blood, Water, Wind, and Stone* across the state. Personal thanks to Mia Jensen and Sean O'Malley, Connie Wieneke, and many others for warm hospitality in support of this project, and to the University of Wyoming's College of Education for longitudinal, state-wide support of writing research and outreach programs.

Thanks for the devotion of groups such as Wyoming Writers, Inc. and Jackson Hole Writers for their long-term cultural enrichment of Wyoming through yearly writers' conferences. Via their invitations to serve as a poetry faculty member and guest publisher, respectively, I've enjoyed opportunities to meet and write with new, emerging and established writers. Through those meetings, this anthology has flourished. On behalf of myself and Sastrugi Press, it is our pleasure to contribute a percentage of the profits from this book to the scholarship funds of both the Wyoming Writers, Inc., and the Jackson Hole Writers conferences. Thanks to you, the reader; by purchasing this anthology, you are investing in the future of writers in this great state.

There is much to concern us in the tumult of today's world, but I do believe that a society willing to bring together its words and voices for the common good is yet a formidable presence, even in the darkest of hours. Thank you for being a part of this book, and of this coming together of voices.

—Lori Howe, Editor

Introduction

During the early stages of this anthology, I was on a tour of Wyoming as a ThinkWY Humanities Council scholar. I spent quite a lot of time considering the book's title, which I wanted to embody the vivid, often ferocious edges of Wyoming, a state so filled with beauty and extremities of nature. I thought about it while I spied on moose in the willows outside Wilson; while I sat next to the stone fireplace in the Sheridan library, and on a wooden bench in the Green River cemetery, considering what it means to live at the intersection between human lives and needs, to mingle our ephemeral blood with the shaping forces of water, wind, and stone. A strong spiritual connection to the power of nature runs through this anthology, as in Lynn Carlson's essay, "Vedauwoo Sketch:" *The aspen lure me into their grove by dropping gold coins on the path. When I step inside their shivering cathedral, I am shushed. "Lissssten," they say.*

Wind, known for its history of inciting madness, is also our neighbor, described in Susan Austin's "Land and Bones," *as if the wind was an intruder, or someone lost, or someone lonely.*

This healthy respect for nature's power is echoed in Rose Hill's poem, "Plains Visitor:"

> Some force unseen compels me here
> to bow in awe as if
> standing too tall
> I might be crushed
> by the weight of sky.

Wyoming is filled with long, silent stretches of prairie, mountains, and a red desert filled with sand dunes and the fossilized past. It is perhaps this vastness which urges us to stop and contemplate our place in this landscape—and what we have to offer to its care. While Wyoming's four-legged, finned, and winged populations do not speak human languages, an intense kinship runs through these poems and stories, as in Susan Marsh's essay, "A Heart in the Shape of a Bear,"

> The mother bear was observed dragging her young one off the roadway into the willows. Is this not the same thing any of us would do, trying to remove our babies from harm, or at least to spare them the indignity of having their bodies on display?

I also listened to participants' poems and essays about water and felt how deeply graven this precious resource is in the human landscape of survival—like the rushing of blood through human veins. This reverence for water streams through this book, as in Maria Lisa Eastman's "Thirsty Cows,"

> Amazed, I asked him if he had ever
> plunged his own dry mouth
> down into a lively stream
> so he could suck the blue water into his belly
> had he felt how it softened his hard salt skin
> and when he surfaced
> heart fluttering, and awash
> hadn't he felt his scorched soul come back to life?

Wyoming, and all the people and animals who live here, are engraved by the seasons—by the scouring heat of summer and the long, sub-zero stretches of winter. We are also romanced by year-round skies of gilded sapphire and sunsets like seas of tangerine fish. Every story I heard in my travels lay entangled with weather. These writers and poets spoke of blood shared and blood shed, of opportunities lost and found, of journeys into the hinterlands of forest and heart, as in Jane Dominick's "Grace:"

> Most, I remember
> riding home, how we watched the falling sunlight
> touch each of us briefly, then move on to caress
> every worldly thing so that it glowed in beauty
> for one moment before the dark.

These authors breathed life and history into boulders, grieved the loss of wildlife in the face of development, lay down their hearts at the feet of rivers they'd known their whole lives, and returned to the ancient sentinels of the mountains to find their own truths.

Whatever you love most about this wild and beautiful state, I hope this collection of poems, stories, and essays brings it home for you, as a place of luminous beauty, fearless nature, and perhaps a bit of magic.

—Lori Howe

POETRY

Thunderwing
Bret Norwood

~

Plains,
the horse,
war and sky—

On the ridge of a white man's last stand,
the polyphonic chorale of
gases escaping the gaping mouths of the dead
was one thing but

now the tufts of timothy and redtop
(once some horse's fodder)
sway and bow in alien silence—
no rider,
no hoofthump.

Before the engine,
horses drove the chariot of history.
Fabled cavalries rode
from broad plains to war:
Proto-Indo-Europeans
(first to tame the horse),
Indo-Iranians, Mongols, Turk hordes—
and here, right here,
at Massacre Hill,
Red Cloud's men defeated Feds
and won a war.

Let me tell you what the country's like:
broad-shouldered mountains, royal blue and silver-veined, hoary
like old men with stories of bygone days,
which fall like crisp leaves from dry mouths, are hunched beneath the sky,
a sky that's wide and blank like Heaven's mind.

Ranges nest extensive grasslands, wind or silence. Like verdant coyotes
with lustrous coats, the loping hills loll,
with lupine in the blue and green May grass and gray sagebrush.
Swooping swallows and whitetail dragonflies circle.

"Who is worthy, alive,
of this?"—the thought
of God
above
the country of
enduring blue sky.

Miles away General Sheridan sits
his blue caboose on the Goose Creek confluence,
a basin city and mining town.
A tall midsummer thunderhead
advances in the west,
a bluecoat too, but different legion.
I hear the wind before it hits:
the coal trains, a thousand-count,
and distant thunder.

Rundundunr...

That there is town and here
the sky-fingering finger of the Fetterman marker,
like a marbled dick,
declares a hundred dead—"no survivors"—
denying the enemy even a statistic
(let alone admission of victory).

Now watch as whipping wind reminds the distant city how recent
—and tenuous—are its roots,
reminds the willows too, up-ripping rhizomes
with cracking of wood and bark,
the spray of splinters in crackling storm air,
and, henceforth, hail pummels the streaming streets.

Winged thunder soars.

The best hunting grounds the Crow held,
Lakota conquered on horse,
drove the conquered Crow west and north.

Winged thunder soars.

Carrington came and built the Bozeman forts.
Lakota horsemen rode
to route the Civil War veterans out.

Winged thunder soars.

Lakota should have held the land they won,
but settlers came as soldiers perished.
The Union recalled generals, issued bureaucrats.

Now, nearby, golfshirted investment bankers
golf golfballs into unmarked graves.

I can't relate.

Old retired women wet petunias as
odd-shaped whirligigs on trailer eaves spin.

I can't relate.

A manchild's trucknuts glint at sunset.

...

"Who is worthy, alive?"

A stream of years exceeds a century:
neither survivors now nor victors.

No one rides for whatever cause.
Wind rustles the vacant plains like hair on the pelt of a dead elk
and I wonder what's there to fight for—what's left?

Who can claim the viridescent grass sea?
Hear the wind, the voice that
calls my name of Tamerlane, calls
no one nowhere—no frontier left to pierce with bold deeds.

And I wonder:
what age does one submit, stop wanting more?
Could Crazy Horse grow fat?
Would Red Cloud sit and watch T.V.?—Maybe.
However, I *hope* not and that—
the hope—means *some*thing.
...
Rununun...
...
I care.
I think it means I care.

Over a prairie where
some men of varying, irrelevant morals
long ago bled out and into oblivion,
the thunderbird spreads his light-veined wings.

Tsh! Rundundunr...

Torrential sleet and roaring speech
engulf the plains in gale.
The thunder has no mind to lie.
The thunder has no mind.
There's honest truth in
wordless fury.
Drum and rumble, silver-pinioned
cloudburst, blue bodied bird
above the mountain.

Drumming, tumble, come and bubble
over blue Bighorn peaks.
Teach the children of the storm.

Deny
me not.
A trial, a trail
is given those you choose.
(Who is worthy
alive?)
Astride
this saddle horse
and silver spurred, divide
this world, this gift,
my trial
and trail.
Enduring, undying
fame of the Horseman Ghost,
name of the Native Sky my father,
God of my fathers' fathers:
the western wheatgrass,
the redtop,
the tufts of timothy,
these are your horse's fodder and ours.
So turn your reins and spur my life,
my cosmic mount, to trod
dissatisfaction
beneath your Sleipnir hooves.
Conquer idling
society's senile contentment;
append again the title "the great" to flesh
who, like you, will ride
through fading ages,
achieve
the aim:

to look at life—
to look at life
and give two shits.

Call my name of Tamerlane, call
for tumult—summon
the reckless horsemen,
killers of men
and saviors, called
Caring, stampeding,
back to life.

Whyoming
Michele Irwin

At first glance, a hinterland
more antelope than men
powered by wind that once
drove pioneer women insane

Manic depressive weather
shapes the landscape
gets under your skin
changes your DNA

Born again in Wyoming
sagebrush in your blood
clinging to alkali soil
bending against the wind

This Language Like Hope
Connie Wieneke

On the Teton Glacier the whim of boulders ebbs and flows on pyramids of moving ice and sand, of shifting water and till. Listen. If you can. This place has no regard for us, only for the daily trade in artifacts, washed-up bottles that taunt their coded messages. We play along, assign significance to the toys we find, transforming them to success and failure by turns and inkling. Balsa wings flung from summits. A 1969 Boy Scout Jamboree scarf that a careful mother once folded. The single ski pole, its ferule pointing to somebody else's broken heart? Scratches and spray paint, bolts that quantify the glacier's advances and retreats. The red and blue jacket hauled off, perhaps the still-missing's only coffin. An ice ax, Fiberglass handle wrapped with athletic tape and duct tape; it could've been yours but for the rusted pick. Thirty-six inches of twine looped for a small hanging or that last impossible belay; really the same thing. Galvanized pipe, 5/8 inches in diameter and 15 inches long; there's nothing to which we can thread it, and there's nothing we can drum it against, except abandoned Gaz canisters, about as useful as cairns mistaken for rocks. Climbing webs unslung and twisted, red white and blue. A two-by-four notched with nails and chalk. Who could have thought to make this place habit? The answers keep us puzzling this language like hope, as if we speak not of loss but with sincerity of planting pansies in the ice and moraine, and crocuses, and yellow and white everlastings for next spring, and the ones ever after.

Deer Woman
Autumn Bernhardt

Little Iktomi,
what would I sound like if I told them about the Deer Woman spells you cast?
Dancing on clouds
jumping over five strands of barbed wire in human form…
out on a South Dakota prairie somewhere
like those reservation hitchhikers of other-worldly beauty
hoof marks on the back seats of old cars

What would I sound like if I told them about being led astray and lost in a forest?
Another face growing out of the side and back of your head
skeletons around your lodge always interpreted as someone else's mistakes
about stirring pots of genitals… just like all the old-time stories

What would it sound like if I told them about the magic of Lakota star highways?
Then, they would finally know that I loved you

Little Iktomi, the Deer Woman of my life, my black magic
my bad time from a time before memories
I wish my heart could break in sunlight
I wish it could break aloud
I wish I no longer had to call you… by anything other than your ancient names

"Deer Woman" previously published in slightly different form in *Red Rising Magazine*, May, 2016.

Black Cat Company
Jeanne Hauf

One Night at the House on Beaver Creek Road
Sheridan, Wyoming . . .

Snuggling *Emerson* on a railroad tie
watching bats swoop low
keeping Thoreau in mind—
thinking of *Success*
defined in terms of spirit
like the wind
whisking navy clouds across the
moon-lit sky
defined in terms of mountains.

Later With the Cat Confined Inside—

Cotton caught in a window screen
shines like bug tracks to the
killer cat, still a kitten on this
stormy Wyoming night with
curtains blowing in the crosswind
from two windows at each end.

Summer Remnants
Eugene M. Gagliano

The sky flares an agitated red,
searing flames of scarlet.
Clouds like smoldering embers
simmer in the October sunset,
a silent reminder of
summer's wildfire fury.
Autumn extinguishes
the torch of summer as
black tree skeletons silhouette
the burnt orange horizon,
remnants of nature's fiery temper.

Fire and Water

Aaron Holst

Red Volkswagen into a fire hydrant, water streams from its severed base,
the car's nose smashed in the middle, its front-mounted fuel tank, ruptured,
its gas burning.

Black smoke coats night's ceiling, fingers of flame mirror in the wash,
curl around us and boil away any hope
the driver survives.

We soak the passenger compartment, steam rolls through and quiets
the snap and crackle. Though water from the hose line can save,
death settles in, we cannot apply enough to bring back life.

Fire engine softens its growl, pump winds down, hose lines go limp, collapse.
Tonight, there is no rescue, only a short firefight,
call to the coroner, removal of a body from its blackened cave.

Gawkers gather as we bag him, his stiffened limbs and torso stripped of
clothes and skin.
Muscle and bone lay exposed, we ignore their tugs at hearts, at guts.
We don't call the water guy to stop the hydrant's flow.

Not yet.

This Main Street line delivers over a thousand gallons a minute, but debris
from the wreck
dams it. Our boots slosh through four inches of water and we feel safe, even
baptized by its presence, for three of us on this crew logs his first call with a
fire victim.

The smell of burned, fatty flesh haunts. Months later, grilling pork chops, I
cannot eat,
as if someone pushes play and the video begins, the noise and flames, my sour
stomach,

the oily, slick odor of acrid, burnt death. It takes years before this memory
washes clean,

again, in flowing water, where I fish for finny things with gills,
where I find solace in fresh-caught words that rise,
make their way into poems—

> eggs that grow to fry,
> to minnow, then fingerling then
> liar's tales.

Once in a while,
boots soaked, pants pasted to my legs,
I catch something.

Early August
Dawn Senior-Trask

Flax the color of sky these cold, clear dawns,
rabbit brush smelling of sunburnt sand.
Asters going to tatters, lupine pregnant with pods,
hare-bells bowing like purple-dressed
ladies hunched over their canes—
down here in the sagebrush hills,
these are the final wild flowers of the year.

The creek runs low and nearly mute,
some of its cottonwoods blighted a rusty brown.
In the meadows the haying's almost done,
every day dry and more bales stacked.
The calves are spending their last weeks
grazing with their mothers. It's weaning time
with shipping to follow, but they don't know that.
The mule deer fawns are losing their spots
and the buck pronghorn marks territory
while he puts on muscle for the rut.

The fat prairie dogs stay underground
taking their late-summer nap, and most birds—
the sage thrashers and all the native sparrows,
the warbling vireo and the fly-snatching phoebe—
have gone into silent hiding to molt.
Only the nutcrackers flash down along
the limber pine ridges, their harsh rasping cries
like a sharp ache of forty-below
deep in the raw throat of winter.

A Southfork Sunset
Deborah Schmitt Emmerich

Backcountry campfire mirrored in an autumn sky
    phantom embers begetting scarlet, crimson, and gold
        straggling clumps of tangerine clouds
            blushing beauties, framed, in the cinnamon sun

    Castled peaks on a burnished horizon
        volcanic neck plugs, bonding earth to sky
        a gentle breeze stirs, crisply seasoned
            by snow rimmed granite and green needled pine

    Dusky wrapper of approaching darkness
        sooty tendrils, drifting, amongst froth and flame
        shadows slip across tapered canyons while,
            with measured step, the cooling sun reclines

Lithic
Constance Brewer

I descend to the dig
                        one foot
                                    at a time,
place my boots with care along
                        marked
                        off
                        grid
                        lines.
A fresh page of my sketchbook   flashes
                white as an antelope's rump.
                                        Pot sherds
scattered through the site,
                                    spiral petroglyphs
etched on basalt.   Burned rock refuse
                    among the midden.

Too early for post molds,
late for Clovis,
the leaf-shaped,
fluted points place us in Folsom.
                        Debitage
                                yields a mass
                                    of flint flakes,
                a few blades.
Survey discovers a rock cairn, leading to
                            an abrupt cliff several miles away.

                    Buffalo
                              jump.
In the pit—
               dart,
                    spear,
                         arrow tips,
                              knives—
layers and levels   of bison bone,
                    exposed,
                                   twenty feet deep.
When my spirit leaps my body,
                         let my material remains rest
                         among the relics
of the past,
                    to become an integral element
of plains stratigraphy.

"A Penny for the Old Guy…"

Tom Spence

The mare was bagged up.
Who even knew she was heavy?
We buried the stud last November.
"A parting shot," as they say.

The mare had a reputation,
a prima donna of the pasture.
Ears back, teeth showing:
don't come near.

                         More than
one Romeo's had his slats
caved in for curling a lip
arching a neck, showing proud,
the man told us.

                         Just like the
old fellow at the Cowboy Bar,
a practiced two-step,
charm, wit, anecdotes
about his former self before

his belly slipped, and his pants
sagged with the weight of time;
and the silver buckle he won
at the county fair for not

falling off. "He gets slapped
for daring," the bartender said.
"But, I saw him leave with
A dude woman from Pennsylvania.

"He bragged all winter on that."
When it's cold and blowing
recollection is a conspiracy
toward Spring.

                        The mare dropped
the foal in the draw, in the
last blizzard, in the night;
and imagined it to standing
and nursing, and perfect.

Her Own Time
Myra Peak

Her steel toe boots are laced loosely
to relieve her swollen ankles
from too much beer, too much pizza,
too many cigarettes.

Her toes are scuffed,
bits peeled back
where rocks bucked up
against fresh leather.

The cuffs of her jeans are frayed
from dragging, knees worn from crawling
under trucks, chasing bolts on cold
concrete shop floors.

Her red plaid shirt is second-hand,
although she can afford a new one.
Her hard hat hollows a ring in her hair
that she washes out every night.

Her hands are dry
from cleaning grease
off brakes of haul trucks taller
than her trailer.

Once she was a waitress working overtime,
a secretary for too many bosses,
sewing buttons at a laundry,
and perming old hair.

Now she doesn't have to smile all day
or pray for coins to make minimum wage.
The hands of her watch are set
to the clock at work, not her own time,

and, finally, that's just fine.

A Christmas Carol
Brian Nystrom

Breathe into the morning, the acrid reek of pulp mill steam, woven
with clay and brick and fog into the fabric of sky. Early walk
to the bar, wretched monk, wreathed in last night's smoke,
coat worn thin, fingers clumsy in solstice wind, the raw light
filtered down through sluggish traffic, lank wrists marbled
by the cold. Rain scissored down all night, the eve of the eve
marked russet, last night's wine metallic on the tongue today.
What luck to taste ash-laden air, cedar and larch charred into the inverted
valley sky. No way around, only to cross
the terrible leaden bridge, morning delivery trucks' exhaust,
the crash of silver ice in black water below, tiny spider swans
hurled west to a slate ocean. Then slip through Old Town, safe,
less than a reflection in a pawn shop window,
shade among shadows rubbed wrong.
Remember, Christmas Eve and closing time will come early as December dusk.
Claim your booth, choke the morning cigarette, and begin again.
Draw up the lace cover of tepid draft beer, snuggle into the imaginary glow
of that first shot and count the blessings and curses of the day, your life:
to wake, to drink, to walk wet streets slick with rain,
to dream your childhood Christmas from the sawdust bar,
the oyster's ruby pearl.

Blizzard of '83
Shanna Ferguson

Sleep-crusted dream fresh
eyes gather at the midnight window,
gaze anxiously on the high prairie
that shifts by the hour.
Snow stacks in piles
hard as granite.

At dawn's light,
I survey the scene.
Winds have blown out, silently
I search the corral, counting each
silver-coated mound, assured all
are still standing.

Then,
I look closer
for the tell-tale fog
from icy muzzles.
Death mirrors life
when frozen.

My fingers loosen
rigor mortis hold
from the sill, then grasp
pine logs to coax
life into flame
and begin the thaw.

Three Ways to Paint the Side of a Boxcar
Lindsay Wilson

I. Train

Sometimes this tagger wishes to transcend his own life
like brakemen in the train yard stumbling
for the first time across a mural,
to feel what the viewer feels.

Sometimes he practices his tag on the air
with just his hand, the way Coltrane moved
fingers over keys without blowing into his horn,
until he can spray his name without thought
onto back alleys, mailboxes, trains.

He knows his art's roots: cave paintings made
using hollow bird bones filled with colored dust,
waiting for breath to blow it onto stone.

Because the caps control the spray's width,
he worries about them
like Coltrane worries about reeds—
wants neither the line or note
to bleed into something else.

The sketch of his next mural is Philadelphia, 1943,
where John plays alone, but he isn't Trane, yet.
Tired from refinery work, he practices his horn
in a third floor walk up, but that's not in the picture.
Instead, he blows a note wrong
and a shade of dissatisfaction crosses his face.
From a new reed, he'll trim the slightest shaving
before holding it against the light.
He wants the reed to vibrate perfectly
and imitate the shimmering legato

he loves in Hodges. He's still learning
to shape the music with his hands and mouth,
learning how his breath curves and escapes pure
like a painting leaving on a boxcar—
something made that can't be owned.
This evening the tagger places *Monk's Music*
on the record player, and when the jacket opens
a shower of green escapes. A clue
from his father, trapped in the plastic covering,
from some forgotten late night
where someone must have slurred,
Is this the one with Trane?

It burns as easily as the paper he rolls it in,
and the high casts him back to the seventies,
where he woke to horns and pianos
drifting on smoke. He tried to hear each note,
each muffled voice, until the night turned
its first shade of blue. This evening,
he stares at the album cover on his easel
and thinks this kind of blue is the obvious choice,
but he'll use it anyway,
along with other bright colors,
which look atonal, so tomorrow morning
the piece will look right from his viaduct perch,
and when it leaves, the straining metal will moan
through the wheel's clicks
as the ceaseless human traffic drowns
out the morning birdsong.

II. Restoration

For her, the moment happened
during a lunch rush, the shoulders of busboys,
plates appearing and disappearing
through the clamored traffic of waitresses
when the heavy, two-beat rumble

cuts through Laramie,
she felt the low rumbling in her feet,
then Coltrane flew by, playing his sax
on the side of a boxcar.

He captured the saxophonist blowing colors
so alive he seemed destined to fracture
under the strain, but the tagger gave him
such wild and elongated hands
she imagined them capable of holding back
any pain, and his eyes,
huge and luminous, cast a spell that stayed
just four beats, or two large window frames,
before he exited stage right.

Later her palms touched an entire gallery
of rusting canvases on stalled boxcars,
and when the flaking murals broke under her hands
her hatred of sun and wind began,
and now, when she finds them
shedding a skin of rust and paint,
she knows she must try to stop them from fading.

III. Alibi

Say I hung with the tagger in his Denver studio
listening to all the right jazz records
his father left as he slouched
into a chair and told me to the story
of Miles Davis in Detroit trying to quit junk.
Cliff Brown had invited him to play,
but he arrived in the middle of the set,
trumpet in a brown paper bag,
strolled up to the stage without apology
and played an awful version
of *My Funny Valentine*. Of course,
the tagger said, Miles denied it…said it was all lies,

but it's better to know the truth
and play the standards.

The truth is, if I've stood watch
while the tagger stole spray paint,
or watched while she restored murals
in the train yard at night,
it means I've loved every word they've said,
and I'm an accomplice to petty crimes,
making up stories for a painting
I saw on a boxcar late one evening,
rehearsing a mural of alibis.

Plains Visitor
Rose Hill

I'm more at ease
when my wedge of sky
is cut by mountain peaks
and my sun filtered
through close-ranked evergreens.

A refugee from the plains, once
soothed by the moire
of silver green grass, once
protected by the bowl
of blue white sky; now
I am insignificant, naked
with no place to hide
on this rimless prairie land.

Some force unseen compels me here
to bow in awe as if
standing too tall
I might be crushed
by the weight of sky.

Previously published in *Prairies, Peaks and Skies,* WyoPoets, 1998

Untitled
Burgit Burke

In the morning, the smell of lilacs
the cool wet smell of night still
asleep in shadows
under the chokecherry and underfoot
petaled brick puddled with last
night's rains and flowers

Checking off boxes, cubicles, to do lists
dribble of time, drab day, black and blue
ink, white page, sweet white wine
now that I am older, I count days
losing count, sit amused.
Stretch and smoke, think.

Jonesing for sex, a road trip, time
to sit and paint, smooth cotton
dresses flying when I dance
contentment is rough and warm
flannel and whiskers, a purring cat,
blue sky arcing over arid green

in the evening, eating a nectarine
thinking in two days I will be…
an hour ago I was just driving,
now I'm going somewhere
time tattooed on my wrist,
not inching, not aging.

Richard Shuts the Gate
Matt Daly

I never figured out how to stop her brother
laughing at my city hands. I never puzzled
out why they used barbed wire to secure the barbed wire
gate, unless to test the limits of outside men.
For years my fingers were always nicked and bloodied
from thorned loops of wire holding each pasture gate shut.
Her brother drove and set most of the posts, dug most
of the post holes himself, strung most of the three strands
of barbed wire himself. At the far edge of the west
pasture he left a few of the posts suspended
in air, held by the tension in the wires. At each
gate, a heavier post pounded deep, looped bottom
and top with strands of barbs a little shorter. He
knew these loops were too short but strung them anyway.
They all did. Too short unless you had lived through taut
secrets of a life with cattle in a place where
wind was more constant even than work, than anger
at how the ends never quite met. I leaned with all
my weight, pushed with all my strength in one arm bundled
up close to my shoulder, reached and tugged at the wire
with the other, scraping the barbs over gray wood
weathered after one season in the wind. After
seasons in the wind, I knew they were laughing, not
showing me this meaningless little secret: how
to shut a barbed wire gate.
                              The next day we get sun,
I'll put on my new work gloves, take nippers, a spool
of smooth wire, replace every loop at every gate.
I will remember how she looked, my wife, when he,
her brother, gave in to the softness we all give
in to, how soft his hands appeared, suspended there
between her calloused palms. Once I pluck those last thorns
looped just for me, I will be rid of him for good.

Still in Love
David Romtvedt

A small earthquake tonight, no real damage
but enough to make the ground shift
and the door, loose on its hinges, rattle.

Reading, I'd drifted off and while I'd been
chipping away at the stone of sleep,
it took the earthquake to wake me up.

I walked out into the moonless night
and tried to think about politics and justice,
but it was no go as the earth still trembled.

What about sex? While I feel less the savage
tension of the body, I still love and, as a lover,
feel both more vulnerable and more reliable.

It's hard to separate seeing from wishing. What is
this talking, these words that come from my mouth?
I'm not so much saying them as being said.

The earth has gone still and down the long valley,
some bird is calling, turning darkness to song.
It seems so romantic—this earthquake.

Hope in Early March
Art Elser

The road washboards to the horizon
where an eternity away the arid land
meets a sterile blue sky and is pinned there
by barbed wire, dirty snow, and tumbleweeds.
Power lines measure the road.
In spring hawks, meadowlarks, and doves
will perch on them, but now they are bare.
A kestrel dives for food and climbs,
talons empty. A few cows appear,
their scattered dearth mirroring
abandoned ranches, trailer homes,
and rusting pickup trucks.

A few dozen antelope, spread over miles,
search the prairie for food with such intensity
they don't look up as passing cars
trail rooster tails of dust.

In the distance, a shape appears in the corner
of two fence lines, a black angus cow.
She's just given birth, the blood-red placenta
still hanging. Nearby a teetering calf,
black fur wet from birth and tongue,
falls, struggles back up, finds
its mother's teat, and sucks lustily,
oblivious to winter's desolation.

Originally published in *The Avocet*, Winter 2014.

Opportunity Missed
Renee Meador

I should have picked the tulips.
Surprise blossoms
after four days of rain-snow mix
erupted from old bulbs
previously grazed by deer
to near demise. This cold snowy
April, tenacity bloomed. I cheered
their red and white traipsing the fence line
among the yellows of deer-proof daffodils.
But daffodils do not a deer-fence make
so today I mourn the tulip fodder
that does not adorn my kitchen table.

And chide myself with should haves:
Should have dared
Should have gone where I chose
Should have left when I stayed
Should have pursued so many
now missed opportunities
Should have picked those tulips

Reflection on Heron Pond
Kim Strellis

In Grand Teton National Park
at the pond, a photo taken one sunny day
revealed an unusual perspective.

Hung on the wall, the image in the picture
was the same, right side up, upside down—
identical trees, clouds, sky and water, in reflection.
The illusion teased me to wonder if truth
or undefined reality lay in the tall reeds and lily pads.

Was I firmly planted on the trail or standing in the air?

The perfect union mirrored two realms
allowing the murky pond to reflect sapphire high above—
a mystery, since the pond, not blue at all—
yet from a greater power
on this heralded day, both echoed one and the same.

Adagio
Jason Deiss

I sit in the cleft of this forest
and imagine that my grandmother's
grandmother
sat in this spot.
We watch the evening
crescendo into pastels,
shadowing us in the mountain
that barks our knuckles back.

The Muskrat
Betsy Bernfeld

On May 30th
the sensitive balance
between the thin blue air
and the filmy green
depths of Yellowstone Lake
tipped
and the lake's frozen surface shattered
into a million pieces.

Students
stood on Fishing Bridge overlooking
Yellowstone Lake as it flowed
into the Yellowstone River.
Chunks of ice moved about
like continents, India shoving up
into the Himalayas,
California coast breaking off
and migrating toward Alaska.
A geologist lectured
on changes in the lakeshore
but his students' eyes
were on a muskrat
sitting on the tail of an iceberg
as it sailed full tilt
toward the bridge.

The muskrat
seemed oblivious to close encounters
with other ice and the fact
that he was speeding
away from home. He was holding
some tidbit of food
delicately

in his forepaws chewing
like mad. A small piece
of ice bumped the rat's vehicle.
He was jarred
but didn't stop nibbling.

"Note
how that sandbar looks different now
from when W.H. Jackson
took this photo in 1872,"
the geologist said.
"Here comes a big one!"
a student shouted. Below
them on the water
an iceberg
much larger than the rat's ship
bore down from behind. The rat
nonchalantly faced forward.
"Would warning him
be interfering with natural order
in a national park?"
someone asked
quickly. No time.
Boom.

No one
suppressed a scream.
The muskrat went right
on his nose, his hind legs launched
six inches in the air. Apparently
confused, he jumped overboard
then crawled right back on. Finally,
he looked around, obviously
thinking, "What am I doing here?" Diving
into the water, he swam against the current, dodging
icebergs, back home. He was rather slick

at it but why not just climb ashore
and run along the bank?

"He'll get stuck
if he steps in the soft mud,"
the geologist answered before anyone
voiced the question, glad at last
to contribute
to the day's lesson.

Trash Rewards—Spring Pick-up on the Buffalo Valley Road
Beverly Leys

Three gold onions, one red, all worse for the wear.

A white ceramic bowl kept for its simplicity.

An on the spot invite from _____ Mason
(turned 80) who stops his Ford pickup to hand me a peppermint drop.
I'll take you dancin' in Dubois. You look me up.

Last year's Christmas looping a silver cord around a live pine
while red and gold glass balls, —three large, eleven small—
buried in the brush beneath accompany
the departed spirit of an emptied fifth of hooch.

A glove, or sock, or scrap of clothing shed by the roadside.

A few stubborn butts, regular, and filtered, grope their way
from mashed packs on the grassy margin.

And the cans, cans, and more cans year after year
crushed, rolled, inert proof
of the insatiable Thirst for meaning.

after a summer of horses,
Jordan Rich

there, strong was to be a rope bucking the
wind saying fuck yes

lariat strong opening wide, wide open

driving away down the 101 south with the bite of sage still in my
hair wondering if I can keep this wild horse healing tangled within
me

after the taste of hay has left my skin
calluses fading from my inner thighs
now

how the heart is a muscle that is tougher up there in the snow on Atherton at
9,000 feet
where the oxygen is skinny

how maybe strong can't go with you when you leave

Frigid
Chris Valentine

Birds at the feeder are fat with fluffed feathers. Steam from the nostrils
of grazing deer turns to frost across the morning breeze. Snow crunches
underfoot as I walk out at zero. Mid-day the temperature hovers around seven.

the smell of my chai

transports me to distant lands

spice of illusion

We wake in the night with no power. He worries about lack of heat. I pull the
comforter closer. Move nearer to his warmth. The logs of the cabin crack in
the frigid air. Deer bump against the bedroom wall as they move into the yard
to shelter.

I savor a book

that tells of hot fireplaces

hands warmed by teacups

He puts on hat and gloves. Ventures outdoors to check the level of fuel. Then
calls and orders more ready for the blast of Siberian air coming in from the
west. Yes, it will be colder this week than last, says the weather forecast.

a friend comes to call

bears a bulb ready to plant

blooms in time for spring

As the temperature descends, I read garden catalogues.

Coyote Encounter
Diane Egge

We were there before the dawn,
in the fog.
Eyes emerged,
unexpected, foreboding.

Eerily, forms
appeared and disappeared,
encircling us.
Outnumbered, nerves tingled
up and down our spines.

Would these shadows attack?
We hoped not.
Obscurely, we spied their acquisition.
Step by step
we eased from their elliptical.
The coyotes stayed with their prey;

The cloud faded, sunlight seeped through,
relief with it.

Spawn
Carolyn Castano

Dark surface
       reflective first element
beneath the mirror egg hearts aching
       heat
Spawning seaweed flow
glimmer minnow, silver fish
shallows and stones and stream
earth and sky bridge
Spider and crane and lamb
       Heat
       Dearth
       Rain

Kayak on Spring Run-off
Lyndi O'Laughlin

It's a small boat I'm in, a thumbnail really,
spit down the Shoshone as if a tongue
were trying to separate itself from a seed,

and there is a lichen-covered boulder
squatting in the middle of the river,
at its base a muscular current,

like a toilet flushing, and it threatens to
block any forward progress I might be
entertaining in my mind, sucking me

and the kayak closer and closer
until I can't help but notice the tiny
snails attached to the rock;

they must think I'm one of them,
just another snail hauling her house
around on her back.

The boulder has a deep voice,
and he pulls me up alongside and asks
if I will stay here with him forever;

tells me that he knows how hard
I have tried, and asks me if I am
maybe growing a little exhausted

from all my clamoring for approval.
I jam my paddle in his eye to free myself,
and think of you, what you asked me

on that last day before I left you
standing on the porch—
"What's wrong with you?"

The Sound of Flight
Linda Ruhle

A great whooshing fills the air,
like a huge blanket vigorously shaken,

as the synchronized flight of 500 blackbirds
swoops into the towering cottonwoods.

Their noisy chattering cacophony and raucous
vocal enthusiasm drowns out the rustling leaves,

buzzing insects and a barking dog. Three shiny
obsidian feathers flutter down, morning gifts.

After a few glorious deafening moments,
like a school of fish gone airborne,

they lift together in perfect unison, a wave
of 50,000 black feathers that fly as one.

Two Ocean Creek
C.F. Kelly

The stream
sings over stones
smooths sand
where rainbows spawn
in shallows
over translucent red eggs
that will soon hatch
fingerlings.

It is beginning its journey
soon leaving pine shade
to hurl down mountains
then relax
in flatland rivers
flowing slowly
to the Atlantic
to the Pacific.

http://wondersofwyoming.com/two-ocean-creek

Showers
C.C. Russell

Something hits the air outside of Cheyenne—a burning scar across molecules of sky. Something heats itself through friction to the point where it combusts, becomes pure energy. This is how your story begins. Your head turns towards a meteor flashing in an arc over the horizon and you breathe nostalgia.

August—summer ending and you sing "American Pie" sitting on the beach of the reservoir while stars fall through a cloudless sky. Your two best friends harmonize. Two years from now, you will no longer know where they live. Two years from now, a frozen chunk of space gas will light your vision on fire and you will come back to this beach, this moment, the chorus ending, your hand bringing the long sweaty neck of a Budweiser bottle towards your lips. The harmony fades slowly, like any good pop song. You flicker in and out of time.

Perseids. You're on a blanket while she reads T.S. Eliot aloud. She is afraid. You are afraid. Both of completely separate ideas. Lines of The Wasteland tilt out over the fields of dry weeds while the sky lights up like the Fourth of July. You count burning trails, try to breathe calmly, quietly, to yourself.

Outside of Cheyenne, you come back to yourself, to the sound of hushed voices. Only the one shooting star and this is not a night for McLean or Eliot. This is a night for the warmth of whiskey and Wish I may, wish I might. This is a night moving slowly enough for the ghosts of time to catch up, for you to rest.

Outside of Cheyenne, voices filter through the air. Something burning its way towards being grounded. Outside of Cheyenne, for a second, you believe it is better to fade away. Outside of Cheyenne, you are remembering.

This is how your story begins.

"Showers," previously published in Riding Light Review

Wyoming 1949
Patricia Frolander

Five hours' ride into the storm,
Old Joe thrashes through drifts, slows,
head down and back humped.
His thousand pounds of horseflesh stop,
quiver, collapse,
almost buried in the whiteout.

I pull myself from the saddle,
flounder, fall against the dead body.
Throat constricts as my knife cuts the cinch,
razor-edge separates the sorrel hide.
Crimson spreads, melts the snow beneath.

Tears freeze as I empty Joe's cavity,
crawl into the steaming breach
hope I'm found in time
to give Old Joe a righteous burial.

Water.
Vicki Windle

Both singular and plural.
Colorless translucent.
Reflective prismatic.
Shape-shifter.
She pours life into willow, cedar, pine,
lizard, sparrow, mink,
sculpts stone with ice blades
and shimmering washes.
Without her we are

Grace
Jane Dominick

In this photo
three friends form a human pyramid.
Two kneel for the third; all smile for the fourth
who holds the camera and the horses.

The background shows
the blue Wyoming sky, a wisp of cirrus clouds—
mares' tails—over golden grass, grey sage
and far-off mountains, vague as an illusion.

I study it,
bring back one sunny winter day,
riding across prairie through that sweet sage,
our horses warm beneath us,
a rhythm easy as our talk and laughter.

Most, I remember
riding home, how we watched the falling sunlight
touch each of us briefly, then move on to caress
every worldly thing so that it glowed in beauty
for one moment before the dark.

Reservoir's Riddle Haikus
Sue Wilcox

Koan: "In the trees fish play,
In the deep sea birds are flying."

Sun blasts the near shore
sere earth cracks and splits its skin,
shingling in bright pain

Cormorants dive deep
spear dank water, sweep bright fish
into long barren haunts

whose moss ridden woods
conceal the silt clogged cabins
left from old folks' youth

while long drowned treetops
freed from algae's grasp, surface,
embrace life's heat, breathe

Smoke Signal
Barbara M. Smith

Squinting against the setting sun,
We see a single wisp rising straight
out of the dark pines.
Is that smoke or a mirage
reflecting off the still water?
Rounding the curve and down the hill,
fire trucks roar past, lights flashing.
Yes, smoke fills the valley,
burns our eyes, that fast.
We can't see across the lake
where we have been.
Fire has found the mountain.
A bullhorn blares from a truck
You're safe, don't worry.
Smoke tells another story.
I walk through the house
filled with the years we spent there.
If we must flee, what would I take,
what would I leave
for the fire?

Last summer on another mountain
two old lovers sat on their porch
watching a plume of smoke drifting across
the dry California valley.
Assured by firemen it was too far away to harm them,
but by nightfall they would flee,
fire leaping across their path on the red hot winds.
Their cats hiding who knows where
in the peach orchard.
Later they breached the barricades
before it was safe, not to fight the fire,
not to stop the barn from burning

or the grove from scorching,
but to search for cats,
eyes glittering through the haze,
surviving.

My grandmother was a girl when the fire came,
burning her house and her father.
He saved them all but the flames snared him
on his way out the door.
They rolled him in cotton batting and he died
swabbed in a white cloud she would never forget.

She looks down at me from the portrait
hanging on my wall. Old eyes in a young face.
I would rescue those eyes from the flame
on my way out the door.

Thirsty Cows
Maria Lisa Eastman

Once I heard a man claim a crazy thing
standing up in front of his slide
mainly addressing a scholarly audience,
he said without a doubt
and at a significance level of point oh five
he had proven that cows didn't need to drink clean water.

He told us that it turns out thirsty cattle
trailing over clay-cracked earth
towards a glint of moisture in the distance
might just as well turn down an ochre road
and sink their burning noses into stone-colored water whose surface
is wreathed in bitter oil and slicked-up mud.

Amazed, I asked him if he had ever
plunged his own dry mouth
down into a lively stream
so he could suck the blue water into his belly
had he felt how it softened his hard salt skin
and when he surfaced
heart fluttering, and awash
hadn't he felt his scorched soul come back to life?

I don't think a cow is any different
from a fish
or an eagle, a willow or an ash.
A cedar, a lamb, a spider or a swan
not too different from us either.
Because what we all need is basically the same—
start with just a good drink of cool clear water.

Ode to Goose Decoys
Michael B. Riley

You were
paper plates
in 1966
held down
by a dirt clod.

I was
a skinny
high school
poor boy
in need of meat.

In college, 1971,
I found your
papier-mâché
and cardboard cutout
cousins, fifty cents each,
at a garage sale—
you were good
until it rained.

After six months
at my first teaching job
I bought
a dozen fiberglass
Gander Mountain shells,
so cracked and split
thirty-six years later
four with lost heads,
I sold you
at a garage sale—
fifty cents each.
Now I live

with a formidable flock
of full bodied Bigfoots,
flocked heads
welcoming eyes
feathers that never freeze—
twenty-four dollars each,

and I am fat.

As I plant the thought of you on the earth
Caridad Woltz

Dearest; I gave a native juniper your name,
it stands close to a tiny bench where I sit for hours,
and hours, sometimes days,
not wanting to end our conversations
so brimming with sound-smiles and wink-memories,
thought-hugs, and endless mountain showers
that wet us both the same.

Why give a tree the name of Isabel?
Like you, queenly in form yet commoner in sound,
at first with Isa to articulate,
you force-bend lips to smile
and then let tongue touch upper palate,
bel, the private place, where no one else
may enter but your own.

Look at how you've grown, three inches in one summer.
Where do you get that love of earth, that strength
as we know-it and never imagined it could stretch,
yet also not-know-it and always hoped to create.
What it forms is doubt in the head that's open,
and widens the schism between the head and brain,
as knowledge molecules are much too large for mind-games.

Inform the head, and leave the mind for minutes at a time,
enforce mind-doubts and rejoice in mind's distress,
for mind doubt needs the practice of disdain from lack
of claiming first and only place. Let thoughts land on human heads
like bees to flowers, or better yet like sparrows let thoughts nest
in decussate leaves to later feed on juniper berries,
or watch them dance like wind midst corn silk manes. Let mind rest.

Sitting by you feeds my doubt that you are gone; your scent,
your hair-tossing ways, your crooked smile, your head's assent,
your quiet thoughts, your strength, all and every form that you can take.
Most noticeably your stance and loyalty to where you're planted,
your native self, your subtle blooming ways, not asking for moisture
yet soaking up erect so that your root not lessen its hold on the earth,
erect also to wind with arms outstretched, yet to my touch you bend.
My head tells me this is how you renew yourself,
you peel back your bark sometime in the summer
revealing darker flesh capable of withstanding winter's distress,
not attached to the old, while not celebrating the new
for the new will be old some day.
Renewing is Revealing. Revealing is Renewing, nothing more
than the work of growing season after season, and starting again.

Strength found in peeling. Prayer found in doing.
      Love found in being yourself.
Lesson learned. Yours truly, if you will have me sit by you sometimes,
      my Isabel.

Canoeing on Saturday
Susan Vittitow Mark

I want to wear this day
raindrop rings on pale olive water
circle upon circle
spreading, joining, fading

I want to wear
fuzzy, waddling, gold-brown goslings
silver trout breaking the surface
yellow warbler—an egg yolk in flight
slicked umber otter swimming
within an oar's-length

"Three yards of this fabric, please."
The clerk grasps the bolt by its clouds
water splashes against her fingers
ducks scatter before her scissors
geese honk in the crisp paper bag

I spread the lake on a table in a sunny room
pin brown tissue pattern to shoreline
run shears down grassy sleeves
roll tracing wheel along the darts that slip
between willows and snags
match front side to front, set a 5/8" seam
I sew a sheath of rain

At the party, the hostess takes my hand
"That dress is beautiful," she says
"Oh this?" I smile,
"I'll have it forever."

Remnants
Teresa Griswold

A pronghorn towers over a tiny calf
drenched in forest whispers.

The pale valley of sage
with a silver river sliding through it
perfumes the air
with a damp, calming, cooling
earthy musk.

Mist rises.
Stillness descends.
Moon rises
in a still light
blue night sky.

Winter Archipelago
Lori Howe

Mindless of time,
these last few mammoths
stood still
until their stories turned
to salt,
written in heat and water
on the inside
of their igneous skins,
before they hardened,
immortal.

In softer seasons,
humans come—
fragile, bright and tiny
as beetles—
to try themselves
against the placid stone.

In winter's quiet,
footed by untouched drifts
and beaver dams closed up tight
against the cold,
Vedauwoo gazes
out across the plains,
a fine gauze of blowing snow
softening the world
back to an ancient sea,
lost to all but these elephant islands
and their long memories of water.

February: Invention
Shelly Norris

Brittle is the visible world
encrusted in white shell—
a cryogenic egg awash in cold
mist and mystery as if born of dull
arctic light. Inspiration whispers amid
crystalized air, pulls

me aside, prompts me
to consider
giving more thought
to thinking about theories,
ideas, the invisible
bones of things.

Probably best to avoid promises,
definitive language, projects
which certainly will be interrupted
by the absent sun's untimely return—
an unwelcome blue schism
of this battleship sky.

Or, if not that, then later, precocious
daffodils or premature tulips plugging
taut buds of false starts through slush
banks into my resolutions.
I've no use for thaw and melt.
What good comes of runoff? Ice jams.

Rivers swell. Established creek beds wash out,
and the cycle of waste and want begins again.
One more frenzied season of green-
bladed renewal, as if we could forget
the last passionate reenactment of sacrifice
and resurrection.

I hear that in the water beneath Antarctic ice
pulsing slowly and left to its own, life
grows five times larger; sea spiders
the span of an adult human hand, jellyfish
rotund as oil barrels. Look about:
Snow-ruffed evergreens support oppositional ravens,

contentious magpies and auburn squirrels nest
in antique cottonwoods bearing their nakedness
toward this cold slate ocean of sky melding
into the ice-edged horizon. Here, suspended
in frost and inseparable from the cold white earth
is where the solid things winter.

Natural History
Carol Deering

Spring surrenders to lambs and wolf pups
and every shade of green. Mountains still
in white headdresses, the clouds
roil and reel in April heartbreak,
blind to the boisterous rush of June.

Songs of squabbling cultures rise.

Pines and willows feel a shaft of sun,
the hush of horses dreaming victory,
birds stake claim to branches, history
ready to repeat or redress.
The moon,
a lens on the river,
reads the weather in our eyes…

The Storm
Tammy Dominguez

Day—heavy as a pear tree
in the heat,
draws the moisture
from your brows and upper lip.
Sky—clear, blue, dreamy,
speckled with downy clouds.

Then
darkness comes
slinking across the horizon—
a sly predator.
The heat of the day kisses the coming coolness
without a marriage.

Soft, gentle white clouds dance
hesitant steps
with swirling, grey intruders,
scales shimmer high above—
fish swimming in the shallows.

Heavens growl,
lightning cracks in the distance,
and rumbling thunder punches
you in the gut:
exhilarating terror, incredible expectation;
fear and hope, anxiety and peace.

The first drop falls,
joined by a flock of fluttering raindrops
to coat your skin like wet lace.

You stand, invigorated
by the singing in your veins,
the fresh, clean scent of rain,
cool, wet water
washes your face and shoulders
and runs for the ground
in rivulets.

Day is chased away by the storm,
shaking out a sparkling carpet
to mirror the sky
for the coming of night.

Moose Bell
Carrie Naughton

Hang out with me awhile,
because it's cold this evening
and the sunset's promise of alpenglow
might remind us both
of summer.

I'll sit on the stoop,
keeping my distance
while you pretend to be a giant piece of yard art,
and we'll watch the clouds
scudding over Teton Pass.

Swaybacked mangy madame,
twig eater, willow bark grinder,
how many seasons have those long greyfurred gams walked you
through lily ponds and over forest snowdrifts
to my driveway tonight?

Big deer, may I call you
Dendi, Dinjik, Æîts'é, or simply...Cow?
I want to make a confession to you while you glance
over your humped shoulder, those cavelike nostrils flaring
at the unforgiven scent of me.

I'll tell you how a friend once informed me
with cheerful, innocent candor
that I'm bound for hell because I don't believe
a god exists who would cleave this world into
the saved and the damned.

And here you are, proof descended from the Pliocene
against any god-concept, yet still partly mystery.
Bearded lady, let's have a chinwag about your throaty fur pouch
and you can explain to me its unknown purpose.
Or not. Some secrets are yours alone.

But I beseech you
to be damned alongside me
and you can ring that bell, your hoarfrosted dewlap moose bell,
because hell's bells, the shape of you
defies all Truth, and I rejoice at that.

Visitor Center

Jennifer Stewart Fueston

Jennifer Stewart Fueston

They suppose what we desire is science,
a shiny but precise display of facts

arranged around the room with charts and buttons,
labeling scientific names of native plants.

Why then these summers later I forget
everything except the photograph?

Shoshone girl, her dark eyes meeting all
our tourist glances as we read

how rivers wound their way through legends:
Yellowstone and Snake caught in a basket,

coyote, spilling them on land,
so they forever flow from one another,

north or south, from this spot where they began.
Her dark eyes scold, or maybe pity me

for not seeing as she did the osprey arc,
golden valleys, great blue-bearded heron

still and solemn on mid-river rocks.
Instead they are relentlessly explained.

We walk amid this place but do not name it,
we sleep here, but we do not dream.

Hannah —
~ give voice to
your own
amazement ~

Covered in Quiet
Melissa Snider

My father flipped the boat
on its belly, slick into the lake.
Dip, pull, lift, trails of drops
left tiny wreaths on the surface.

If we talked, it was about the plain day. Another
blue sky, the pines, breath of woodchips
and mud exhaling. Maybe he told me
how, as a boy, he earned the right
not to wear a lifejacket by learning
to swim across the lake.

I could swim only to the platform,
breathless if I looked too long
at trunks below, stretched
from known to unknown
where water turned cold and black.
Imagine the journey across,
skin of pollen parted for my bare arms
thinking of nothing but breath
and forward, and not
of the deep.

Surface split by our boat, quickly healed
in its wake. Words spoken, then
covered in quiet. Paddles hit bottom,
snagged a tangle of lily pads before the bridge.
Hoping for crayfish, we pulled cages
by chains twisted with stems
up from the visible bottom.

I don't know whose fault it was
but we leaned at the same time, either

to gather a trap, or reach
for something fallen. Slow motion approach
of surface, then submersion sped our disorientation—
flailed arms and mouthfuls of water in spite
of our shallow swim.
We stood, my father up to his thighs
and me to my waist. Laughter lapped
over the shock, sudden as the hammer
of a woodpecker's beak.

We counted to three
and turned the canoe, stepped dripping
into its cheerful bob and pull our paddles
toward home. Pooled in the bottom
of our boat, water mirrored the sky, our ordinary
conversation, our unexpected
baptism.

Whose Land?
Cindy Jackelen

November 11, 1862, Henderson, Minnesota

Yellow Bird

Long has valley been home
to Mdewakanton Dakotah people,
gift from Wakan Tanka
since time immemorial.

Long has Cansa' Yapi river flowed,
where waters reflect the sky
cleansed and nourished us,
lifeblood of The People.

Long have the animals
sacrificed their spirits
that we might eat
and be clothed in their skins.

Long have we trod
these prairies and hills,
moved homes with the seasons,
shelter for each time.

Wilhelmina

Boarded a ship,
Left behind family and all that's dear
for new land in
America.
Knelt and kissed the earth,
swore I'd never set foot on a ship again.
Packed steamer trunk and toddler,

Rode rails west
to unseen destination, cholera
claimed all we had left.
Paused long enough
to bury her on a bluff,
moved away from disease
to newly opened treaty land,
verdant river valley.
Staked our claim, 160 acres,
rich black soil,
first white settlers here.
No time for loneliness,
built this farm with
hard work and grief.

Yellow Bird

Wasi'chu come to this land,
speak of Great Father
who wishes us to
make our mark on paper,
live on reservation land
we will own.
How can I know which
piece of air is mine to breathe?
Cut our hair,
wear white man clothes,
take up plow,
raise cows in fences.
Never again to follow bison herds,
never again to follow rhythms of Mother Earth.
Offered money we can't eat,
food locked in stone houses.
Rain does not fall,
children moan with hunger.
He who speaks for the Great Father
tells us to eat grass or dung.

Little Crow seeks peace
but tempers flare,
young men,
hungry,
battle for our land.

Wilhelmina

Baking bread to feed my children,
open door cools my sweat.
Glanced up, two redskins,
scared me half to death.
Fed them,
told them to leave.
Frederick speaks of discord.
Indians won't abide
by 1851 Treaty.
Sleepless nights of heat and fear
of losing everything again.
Women and children
shelter in barricade, guarded,
men go off to battle for our land.

Yellow Bird

So many lost.
Old men, women, children
gathered at Camp Release,
scared, confused,
guarded by white soldiers.
Where are our warriors?
First babe born on moonless night,
cold eats us,
deep hunger in our bellies.
Herded like cattle
across brittle prairie in
Moon of Rutting Deer.

Prodded by soldier man,
keep moving, weary.
Wasi'chus line villages
taunt us, proud people
broken.

Wilhelmina

Defeated.
Hang them,
rid this land of
murdering savages.
Good riddance.

Henry

The injuns are coming!
Real injuns
dressed in skins and blankets and shame.
Like a parade,
Main Street crowded,
angry populace cursing,
screaming, shouting, crying,
armed with guns, knives, clubs,
we throw sticks and rocks and hate.
Frank's mother, enraged,
snatches nursing babe
from Indian mother
dashes it to ground
spilling blood,
stabs at her with scissors,
crowd cheering,
soldiers drive the crowd back,
hurry through town
as fast as they can.

Yellow Bird

Oh my babe, my heart,
torn from my arms,
your smile drains in the dust,
cuts bleed my sorrow.
Paused long enough for
cherished tribal custom,
death ceremony,
laid away in crotch of a tree.
Pushed on to camp of misery,
Fort Snelling.

Wilhelmina

Only good Indian
is a dead Indian.

Henry 1941, Birch Coulee Monument, Morton, Minnesota

Old man's memories burn.
Shame.
Dakotah treated like cattle,
robbed, butchered.
Horror at my own glee.
Whose land is this?
Bought with blood,
tilled with broken promises,
plowed under prairie and traditions.
Essence of the Dakota lost
to white man's ways.
This stone
to honor and perpetuate
their names
forever.
What honor?

NONFICTION

Requiem for a Desert Elk

Erik Molvar

[handwritten: Good luck with your own writing! Erik M...]

"Where'd you get that, grandpa?" asked the youngster, pointing to the heavy-antlered elk skull hanging from the front porch of the cabin, slowly bleaching to dust. It had six points on each antler, and a brow tine drooped straight down from one thick beam before curving forward. "Found it out in the Red Desert," the old man replied absently, and the two returned to their cribbage.

* * *

The drop-tine bull was born high on the slopes of the Oregon Buttes, where a north-facing couloir trapped just enough moisture to foster a stand of aspens. Before him stretched a sea of sagebrush, dappled by pink and white mantles of phlox and tinged purple with lupine and larkspur. The windswept rims curved downward toward green swards of wiry grass, and thorny greasewood gathered in flats where alkali salts collected. The desert was verdant today, in mid-June, but soon the grass would cure off to a tawny brown. Soon the late spring thundershowers would dwindle, and skies desiccated by the furnace blast of summer would stir up choking dust. But on this day, the newborn calf plopped wetly into cool green grasses, among tree trunks carved with graffiti nudes from long-ago sheepherders. Licked clean by its mother, the calf wobbled to its feet, instinctively squeaking for its first taste of milk.

This calf was born at the right time, just as spring greens rose up at the peak of early growth, rich in nutrients. As summer progressed, the succulents would dry out, their nutrients depleted. Thick walls of cellulose would make the dried and cured grasses and wildflowers harder for a four-chambered stomach to digest. For now, though, the mother elk's milk was rich and grassy with nutritious new growth.

This was a solitary time. The dam would stash the young calf beneath a tall sagebrush or in a cluster of chokecherry shrubs, white spots and an absence of scent keeping him hidden from coyotes and the vigilant eyes of golden eagles. Off his mother would wander, sometimes half a mile or more, where she could fuel her need for high-protein forage while drawing the attention of predators away from her offspring. Day after day the calf was left alone, curled beneath a sagebrush on the high slopes of the butte. Below him stretched a landscape seemingly unchanged for a thousand years. The young elk could not know that for eons, small clusters of copper-colored two-leggeds had huddled in shelters of brush, and later in conical lodges of hide, in the sagebrush below. An attentive eye could still discern rings of stones to mark their tipis and ancient hearths.

These inquisitive beings chipped stones into sharp tools and made fire for their own purposes. Too slow to catch larger animals by speed, instead they used guile and cooperation, building drivelines of stone to funnel prey off low cliffs. After ten thousand years of wandering afoot, a new and speedy form of transport arrived at the lodges of the two-leggeds, in the form of horses traded or captured far to the south. The horse evolved in these arid steppes, but vanished entirely from the continent during the Ice Ages. Mastering horsemanship, the tribes became mobile and aggressive, and better able to pursue the herds of the great woolly bison. Trade with tribes from the trackless boreal forests of the north brought the arrival of thunder sticks.

The Cree were in contact with a new, pale tribe of French-speaking two-leggeds who sought the pelts of beavers and other soft-furred animals. In trade, the Cree obtained trinkets and technology, including thunder sticks that could fling a tiny lead projectile with deadly force. The ancestors of the drop-tine bull experienced the coming of the horse and the thunder stick to the bands of two-leggeds as a real threat; in former years, elk were killed only occasionally, when the two-leggeds took them by surprise. But this flourishing of the horse culture among the indigenous two-leggeds would prove as brief as it was glorious.

In the distance, the snowy crags that would be called the Wind River Range rose beyond the sagebrush gap in the Great Divide that would come to be labeled South Pass. Through this gap poured caravans of ox-drawn contraptions, lurching across the divide with cargoes of pale-skinned two-leggeds. These foreigners brought with them deadly diseases, dreams of empire, and an acquisitive drive to own and dominate the land. But the young calf marked none of these comings and goings of primates on the sagelands below.

From where he lay, evidence of the two-leggeds and their dominion was nowhere apparent. The extinction of great herds of buffalo, the dis-appearance of the wolf, the great bear, and the mountain lion to make way for dim-witted herds of cattle and sheep, the near-disappearance and subsequent repopulation of the fleet pronghorn, all these things had come to pass long before. The young calf nestled in a succession of shady hideaways, growing rapidly on its mother's milk, receiving visits from pygmy rabbits peering out from the sagebrush, flitting songbirds with their melodious mating calls, and the occasional burrowing owl turning its head around backward to peer at the dappled young mammal in his shady depression. For the elk calf, the world was new.

* * *

Soon strong enough to travel, the elk calf joined its mother in ever-ex-panding forays across the sagebrush. Before long, the solitary pair joined other females, some with calves. Theirs was a loose-knit herd, sometimes numbering eight, sometimes twenty, sometimes thirty-five. Coursing across the desert at a lope, the herd flowed like liquid bronze through secluded draws and over windblown rimtops. At times they penetrated a maze of finger ridges and canyonlets, named the Honeycomb Buttes by the two-leggeds. Banded in vermilion and unearthly green, these badlands gained their hues from trace iron deposited when these arid wastes were the receding waters of an ancient lake, 50 million years in the past. The rapidly-growing youngster had no way of knowing that the gray-blue hexagons of stone that crunched under hoof were fossilized tiles of ancient turtle-shells.

At dawn and dusk, the herd ventured across the flats of the Big Empty, moving quickly and silently through greasewood patches of dry washes to gain elevated terraces or stabilized dunes where nutritious foods could be found. But in the light of the full moon, or in the height of day, the herd sought shelter among the scattered aspen groves or chokecherry bushes along the Bush Rim, or sought out tall sagebrush beside Alkali Draw or Parnell Creek. Finding someplace to hide in such an open landscape was a constant challenge. Every minute in the open, grazing on nutritious grasses, fattened the cows and enriched their milk, but also increased the odds of a coyote pack being able to pick off a careless calf.

The real danger came when the herd wandered near the ribbons of gravel built by the two leggeds' monstrous machines. One clear summer morning, the herd flowed up from a hidden draw onto the tablelands, and an oilfield truck towing a tank of wastewater thundered up over the crest at the same time. There was a loud blast on the horn as the confused elk hesitated, then coursed across the ribbon of gravel to avoid being cut off. The Drop Tine Calf was fortunate this time, being near the front of the herd. But the truck plowed into the animals at the rear, killing two cows instantly, and breaking the hind leg of one young calf too slow in clearing the chrome grille. The stricken calf hobbled three-legged after its dam, while the females in the rear doubled back into the draw below. Those at the front of the herd picked up their pace, seeking the high country of Bastard Butte, leaving the three-legged calf and its dam to fend off the coyotes on their own. So it was that the Drop Tine Calf saw these linear strips of gravel brought noise and fear and death. It was a lesson that would serve him well.

Sometimes the herd's journeys took them far afield, coursing southward past Black Rock or to the lowest parts of the Great Divide Basin. When the Great Divide reaches the Oregon Buttes it splits into two branches, one running south along ancient volcanic flows and high shale rims, the other heading across Continental Peak and eastward along the Cyclone Rim, to the Ferris Mountains a hundred miles in the distance.

Cupped in the basin between the two arms of the Great Divide are over six thousand square miles of sagebrush and greasewood, where cloudburst or snow squall trickles down to the center, evaporating as it concentrated the salts and alkali it picked up from the soil along the way. One dusk, as the fading sun gilded the mares' tails with rosy highlights, the herd wandered through the scattered dunes and then onto the Luman Rim. Here, the mares wandered across bare and salty flats where scraggly saltbush grew, and on into stabilized dunes where the prairie junegrass poked in green clumps between the sagebrush.

The moon rose as the Drop Tine Calf trailed along behind his dam as she grazed, and it was here that the young calf took his first tentative mouthfuls of grass. His stomach ached from the fibrous, foreign matter. But this was eased by licking his mother's muzzle, inoculating the first chamber of his stomach with microbes that would one day grow into an abundant flora to help him digest a fibrous diet of grass after the milk ran dry. The herd drifted east, but crossing a rise they beheld a towering bank of lights, grinding away in the night and spilling forth two-leggeds and a procession of wheeled machines. The great grumbling contraption, probing greedily in a quest for liquid hydrocarbons, was far beyond the ken of any elk. The herd turned back, toward the darkness and quiet, abandoning productive ranges that now were filled with danger.

Fifty miles to the east, a yellow bus disgorged schoolchildren hailing from Ethete, Fort Washakie, and Stevens Point into a clutch of structures hard by a railroad siding and stockyard. Blinking in the fluorescent glare of the meeting room, the copper-skinned children stepped one by one to a podium, began to speak into the microphone, first tentatively and then with growing strength and confidence. They articulated an ancient connection to the land. The oilfields had grown too large, they said, poisoning sacred desert springs and driving off the animals. Each indigenous child offered a unique and powerful voice, and the room was stilled, for a time. Out in the desert, the great metal beasts continued to grind on. The web of gravel and pipelines and drilling pads metastasized, spreading north and west, driving before it reclusive sage grouse and their broods to seek shelter in less productive sagebrush patches far from the rumble of machines.

* * *

It was in the summer of his third year that the young bull grew branching beams of antler atop his head, mantled in velvet-robed skin engorged with blood, beginning to grow into his name. The velvet laid down calcium and phosphorus to form beams and pointed tines, a new weight for the Drop Tine Bull to carry. In August, as the rabbitbrush bloomed brightly with yellow blossoms, the velvet withered and started to itch. The young bull worried at the sagebrush with his antlers until it fell away in bloody strips, revealing pale bone. The antlers were spindly, each an exact mirror image of the other. Joining a bachelor herd of younger bulls, the Drop Tine Bull felt new urges, and tested his new antlers against those of his companions, their sparring deliberate and cautious. When the Drop Tine bull accidentally poked his sparring partner in the eye, his opponent emitted tiny squeaks, and the Drop Tine Bull disengaged and backed away. In this way, the Drop Tine Bull gauged which of his compatriots had antlers too big for him to meddle with, and was able to identify the one skinny bull he could push around.

As summer turned to early autumn, the herd was wandering atop rims above Jack Morrow Creek, when suddenly the leader broke into a canter. The Drop Tine Bull was slow to get underway and lagged behind, and soon a stinging bite hit the bridge of his neck, followed by a loud crack. He accelerated and dropped down from the rimtop, plunging down the steep slopes beyond and into the tall sagebrush of the valley floor. Had the metal object penetrated his neck a few inches lower, it would have severed the thick ligament that held his head upright while he ran. As it was, he suffered only a crease in the hide of his neck, which hardened into scar to mark his brush with a premature death.

With the coming of the first snow, the bachelor herd bumbled into a large herd of cow elk, guarded by a heavy-beamed harem master. Approaching cautiously, the Drop Tine Bull caught a whiff of females in estrus, quickening his blood and dulling his senses. Wandering too close, he caught the attention of the harem master, who charged, engaging the inexperienced bull with the fury of a runaway train. This was no ritual duel: the harem master was out for blood. The Drop Tine Bull wheeled to flee, but the harem master caught his flank with a long tine and ripped a gash from ribs to neck. It would heal slowly, a visible reminder that younger bulls must keep their distance from the edge of the harem.

* * *

After four more winters, the Drop Tine Bull reached the height of his prowess. The great beams of his antlers each carried six long, curved daggers on each side, symmetrical save for the single tine above his right brow. This "drop tine" showed up in his seventh year, and would grow in this way each successive year of his life. The scar along his flank had healed into a pale, broad stripe. His muscles rippled beneath a tawny coat of fur, and his neck grew thick beneath a shaggy collar of blackish hair. Now he was able to best any rival during the pre-rut sparring. Sensing his superiority, he gathered together a harem of his own on the gentle north slopes of Steamboat Mountain. At first, he herded his females too closely, causing them to scatter in aggravation. He learned patience, gathering the harem back together, tuning his ears to the small squeaks and barks that are the language of female elk. Avoiding the gravel fretwork to the south with its beetling machines, the Drop Tine Bull herded his harem to the windblown heights above Chicken Springs. Visiting the rimtops in the evening, he escorted his harem down to the remote valleys of Parnell Creek during the day, where they could remain hidden from view. The females he guarded had a pecking order of their own, enforced as vigorously as that of the bulls.

When the Drop Tine Bull would paw in the soft earth and let fly a stream of musky urine, the dominant cow was always the first to wallow in the rutting pit and coat herself in the scent of dominance. As each cow came into estrus, she became receptive to the Drop Tine Bull's advances. But only the most dominant females had immediate access to the harem master's attentions. In this way, the strongest and most dominant cows could be assured that their calves would be born exactly when the grasses were at their peak of nutrition.

* * *

For successive autumns, the Drop Tine Bull reigned over large harems of females. One hot September day, among the limber pines of the Oregon Buttes, he bugled his supremacy, and was answered by bugling from the opposite slope. He stepped out from the trees to thrash his antlers, now short but with great thickness of age, against a luckless sapling. A flock of Clark's nutcrackers started from a nearby grove in a flurry of wings, as the harem surged forward to maintain contact with their harem master. On the far wall of the bowl, a pale and solitary two-legged worked its way toward the caprock of the butte.

The harem caught wind immediately and moved off southward, but the Drop Tine Bull stood his ground, giving the sapling a fine thrashing, intent on ceding ground to no one. He eyeballed the two legged with a bloodshot glare across the distance of several hundred yards, but the two-legged merely looked back, making no move. Eventually the harem master tired of the standoff, drifting off to his cows.

This would be the last autumn in which the cows would carry calves bearing the Drop Tine gene. The summer had been dry, and by the end of the autumn rut the ribs were showing beneath the harem master's dull, tawny fur.

That winter, heavy snows in the higher desert drove the herd down to the wind-blown gap just north of the Boars Tusk. The elk wandered the wind-rippled dunes to the north of the Tusk, seeking out patches of wiry marsh grass blown free of snow by incessant gales that blew stinging sand and crystals of ice. The Drop Tine Bull was able to hang on through the dark days of February, ghosting up to the windward slopes of Essex

Mountain under a rumpled blanket of cloud. Here, exposed sagebrush provided some nutrition, but although filling, the defensive compounds in the sage prevented his stomach flora from extracting the energy and nutrients needed to keep his 650-pound frame thrashing through the crusted snow. It was late March, and the sage grouse were beginning to gather on their lekking grounds to fan their tails and send out their burbling calls across the sagebrush, before the Drop Tine Bull bedded down one last time, stomach crammed with indigestible brush, and rose no more.

Ravens and magpies gathered in flocks above the fallen monarch, luring in coyotes and badgers able to rip open up the tough old hide with sharp teeth, that the birds might have their share of the meat. By June, the ants and beetles were cleaning away the last scraps, and the skeleton bleached beneath the desert sun, waiting for the bone collector who would spirit away the skull and hang it beneath the cabin eaves, in a silent honoring of the kinship amongst all living things, marked as we all are by the same remorseless inescapability of time.

Vedauwoo Sketch
Lynn G. Carlson

In the southeast corner of Wyoming, in the Medicine Bow National Forest, is an area known as Vedauwoo. Pronounce it "vee-dah-voo" while you visualize castle-sized piles of rounded rock, looming over pine and prairie. I hike Vedauwoo's Turtle Rock trail with my span-triever, Luna. "Hike" might be too energetic of a word. Mostly I wander, amble, scramble and stare.

As we leave the campground and join the trail, a raven's croak announces our arrival. We pass a stand of sagebrush, and I pluck some lacey leaves, pinch and hold them to my nostrils: sweet, herbaceous, a hint of citrus. We cross through scattered junipers and move down into the forest where hundreds of mature lodgepole pine have succumbed to a pine beetle plague. Denuded of needles, they lean where they fell, in the arms of their children.

The aspen lure me into their grove by dropping gold coins on the path. When I step inside their shivering cathedral, I am shushed. "Lissssten," they say.

Deeper in the forest, a bull moose steps from behind a Douglas fir and angles his crown of antlers toward me. I grab Luna's collar and wait, half expecting an Aslan-like pronouncement, but he only nods his great head and turns back to the forest.

Luna and I arrive at Turtle Rock. This formation looks like it was summoned from an ancient sea—a herd of granite manatees that gathered and tumbled down and rolled into place. The trail circles the base, like a moat, flowing through Engelmann spruce and limber pine.

I glimpse troll faces in the gnarled bark of ponderosa pines. I hear a plop in the beaver pond. I see a flash of movement in a cavern's gloom— but it's only a chipmunk who chitters, flicks his tail, and dives under a log.

The light dims, and I look up to see a cloud sweeping the hem of her gray gown over Turtle Rock. In the breeze, I taste the coming snow.

A mastodon-sized boulder balances next to the path, looking as though it will topple down and crush us, although it has stood poised that way for centuries. Luna sniffs at a wart of lichen on its nose. I pause to stroke its pebbly skin.

We step into knee-high broomstick grass. The Wyoming wind waves its wand and the grass bows down as we exit the trail.

Vedauwoo is magic. It's a place that seethes with life, then dies, and is born again, in every rock and leaf and vapor, and I live and die and am born again in it.

The Heart of the Dance
Su Child

The pre-Solstice full moon rose late over still-warm earth. Heart Mountain seemed to lean in, interested in my activities in the bright moonlight. My full-length skirt and Mexican cotton sleeveless blouse were a splendid backdrop in shades of red. Lavender light reflected upward from the clam shells sparkling out from the unpolished silver of my Navajo squash-blossom necklace. The glow seemed to herald this deepening discovery of my Lakota heritage in today's Plains Indian Country. I held my necklace up toward Buffalo Heart Mountain, sacred site of the Absaaloka, the Crow tribal people, and then placed it around my neck.

The lingering warmth of the mid-summer day didn't require a shawl, but I wanted to see my vintage Northern Plains red wool shawl by moonlight, its orange fringe swinging rhythmically as I danced my way out to the meadow. Then, with the shawl extended over the length of my arms, I felt the freedom of bird wings as I improvised Native American Women's Fancy Shawl. Moving spontaneously to a favorite Lakota song, my light-footed twirling extended the shawl's fringe in colorful motion visible in the moonlight as I circled clockwise. The pungent fragrance of prairie sage, and the fresh coolness and sounds of the rushing stream in a nearby canal, enhanced my anticipation of the Plains Indian Museum's annual Pow Wow Opening Day the next morning. Before leaving the meadow, I leaned against the fence, savoring the evening's fragrant stillness. Refreshed, I quietly strode back to the house in the moonlight.

Arriving at the Pow Wow grounds early the next morning, I happily greeted friends and participated in the many preparations. A steady stream of Indian performers and families entered through the roped-off space designated for the Grand Entry. As drum groups, dancers, and family members of all ages settled in under the blue awnings of the arbor, laughter and cheerful banter accented the sounds of rehearsing drummers and singers. Each group quickly assisted one another with the finishing touches of hair and regalia, making certain that every item was well-secured, especially the feathers.

As performers lined up for Grand Entry, I looked around. The audience and M.C. were enjoying getting acquainted, the Indian Market booths were busy with interested shoppers, and children gleefully rolled down the grassy slopes behind the bleachers, into the legs of strolling adults. Looking closer at those in the front lineup of the Grand Entry, I saw Blackfeet Plains Indian Historian and film maker, Curly Bear Wagner, next to the veteran carrying the flag. He carried an eagle in the crook of his left arm. A beloved board member of the Plains Indian Museum, he officiated at each Pow Wow. He'd later take his place near the Arbor Directors and jovial M.C., Lakota 'eyapaha,' Chico Her Many Horses, an educator at Wyoming Indian High School, on the Wind River Reservation.

Curly Bear directed the dancers as they filled the entire arbor. After elder Dr. Joe Medicine Crow's invocation, and as the performers left, I again felt the uniqueness of this smaller, more intimate holistic event, a combination of artistic, spiritual, and athletic competition amongst performers from different, yet fundamentally similar, cultures.

At the end of the teen girls' Fancy Shawl Dance, we experienced one such difference. A feather dropped during that round. Chico called for Curly Bear. While the girls remained in line, Curly Bear came into the arbor with his long prayer pipe. He prayed as he pointed to each of the four directions before picking up the feather. Tribes differ in the handling of dropped feathers. Some dancers claim a discovered dropped feather as good fortune. In this event, a teenaged girl was blessed that day as this gentle traditional teacher returned her feather. We all waited quietly while Curly Bear spoke to the girl and her family about the importance of prayerful meditation before entering the arbor. He told her that this incident was unfortunate, but because she was a member of a dancing family, she would learn to include prayerful attention in her preparation.

Chico then told her that the judges would let her family know later if she could compete the next day. She was dismissed for the first day. All of the dancers, and the audience, were privileged to witness the sacred significance of dance, which exists among traditional tribal peoples today. I treasure those cultural glimpses I experienced that afternoon.

Observing the Men's Traditional competition up close, as the sun's slanting rays highlighted their rhythmic touch-step footwork, is also a special memory. Totally immersed in his dance, one elder caught my attention. For that brief period of time, the arena appeared transfigured in motion, music, and light, creating a colorful array of vitality for the closing of the afternoon competitions.

I accompanied my friend's family to the parking lot, where performers' vans served as dressing rooms to create an outdoor backstage atmosphere. That same elder, with graceful ritualistic movements, was removing and storing his regalia in the adjacent van. I stood back from both men, honoring their space, sensing the ongoing nature of the sacred experience. Suddenly, a vivacious young girl dashed out of the van.

"I'm seven, and I fancy dance," she announced. Her round young body fit snuggly into a soft beige dress, swaying as she spoke. "My mother taught me to fancy dance," she confided, looking up at me, both pleased and proud.

I bent down as I replied, "I love fancy dance."

"I'll dance for you, would you like that?" the little girl asked. Then, she skipped happily to the front of the van. Springing lightly from the pavement, and twirling with one arm raised, she smiled at me as she danced for just the two of us.

I keenly felt the child within me, dancing in those brief moments. The girl's mother, a Jingle Dancer, joined us. Ah, a family of dancers!

While running back to me, my new friend joyfully announced, "I'll be dancing tomorrow."

"And I'll be watching you," I replied just as joyfully, bursting into happy laughter and sharing a big hug.

A Heart in the Shape of a Bear
Susan Marsh

Heartbroken

The only word I could write in the reply post when the news infused Facebook.

The mother bear was observed dragging her young one off the roadway into the willows. Is this not the same thing any of us would do, trying to remove our babies from harm, or at least to spare them the indignity of having their bodies on display?

I imagine her, unable to save him, walking away alone with nothing but a mother's grief. No purpose to the coming days, no small companion to lean and climb and sleep on her, no appetite. The light has fallen out of her life.

The last item in the news report: an adult black bear was also killed that day. Written as an afterthought, a footnote. As if it mattered less.

My Heart Goes Out
To the black bear in the cage.

At the Game & Fish office for a meeting, somebody says, want to see a bear? We look out the window, to where wet meadows and marshes of the National Elk Refuge spread a mile across and butt up against the front of the Gros Ventre Range, the wilderness, doorway to a million acres of wild land where bears roam every day. We might see a bear there, all right; we had seen cougars and wolves the previous winter.

The man stood up. "I'll show you," he said.

We followed him into a dusty high-ceilinged brick and concrete warehouse, where snowmobiles and pickups and an assortment of G&F specialized equipment was stored—trailers with various winches and boxes and barrels welded to their beds, converted to haul dead moose and elk off the highway, fingerling trout from hatchery to lake, and problem bears into the remote backcountry. Six-foot sections of corrugated steel culvert with rebar mesh doors served as transportation for the bears.

One of the culvert traps was occupied.

Caught at the edge of Jackson, between the national forest on the slopes of Snow King Mountain and the neighborhoods crawling up its hem from town, the bear had been hitting on trash cans and bags of dog food stored outdoors in plastic tubs.

The bear had spent the night in the culvert, the rebar door slammed down when it investigated a sample of odoriferous roadkill at the back of the trap. Hours later a G&F officer peered in, saw the bear, hooked the trailer to his pickup and drove it to the warehouse. More hours later, he planned to transport the bear to a remote forest road on the west side of Togwotee Pass. In the meanwhile, we could have a look at it.

It. I chafe at calling another creature "it." Bears come in genders, like people, but I didn't know which pronoun to use. I hung back while the others stared and muttered and leaned in for a closer look. The bear retreated to the back of the trap.

Soon the people grew bored with staring at the bear. As they moved away, engrossed in another conversation, I took a step closer.

As always, I was at a loss for how to approach a wild animal, even one in a cage. I wanted to show sympathy and respect, my movements slow, non-threatening. I gave the bear a quick sideways glance.

I caught enough of a glimpse to see the dark coat, looking dull, as if the bear had been rolling in dirt. The bear was round as a bear ought to be in late summer and sitting upright like a dog.

When I returned to the meeting what stayed with me, what continues to stay with me, were the eyes. Small for its broad face, the bear seemed to be squinting, as if to wish me and the nightmare of imprisonment away. I saw in the expression complex emotions I could not decipher. The bear was safe for the moment, but alert, wary, and puzzled. If I were tempted to give the bear some of my words they would be, "What is going to happen to me now?"

I wanted to assure the bear that it would be released some sixty miles north of the Snow King trash cans and soon it would be snacking its way through a huckleberry patch. I didn't want to think about the chances of it being hit by a car or killed by a hunter or run off another bear's favorite berry patch. How would it fare, in all likelihood, this smallish black bear that looked to be an adolescent, having fattened for a month on the easy fare of kibble and garbage, now fending for itself in an unfamiliar part of the world where grizzlies, known to kill black bears, were king?

I could conjure no good ending to this story.

The Wild Beating Heart of the World

The eyes of the black bear reflected our intertwined history, bears and humans. Part of us swells with wonder at the sight of a bear while part of us wishes they would go away. Bears represent a deep and ancient part of ourselves, a remnant of an animist mythology that reaches into the farthest place within us. Ancient cultures revered the bear, the symbol of death and resurrection. Each year the bear emerged from underground, an auspicious event.

Today we have problem bears and too many of them. Game and Fish talks about reducing the number of black bears by allowing hunters a harvest, as if they constituted a crop and not a population of wild creatures that has thrived for millennia before we came onto the scene. A kill quota is set each year. When asked, no one can tell us exactly how many black bears there are.

Bears are not our enemies, nor are they our friends. They are not cute, semi-tame creatures, even when they allow us to observe them at close range. If they hold wishes in their hearts, these most certainly include a desire to be left alone.

An unexpected encounter with a bear can startle the heart. An emotional remnant from the days of cave men and cave bears, our fear meter ranges from mild surprise to terror. Bears remind us we are not always at the top of the food chain. They attack out of fear, aggression, hunger, or to protect their offspring. We attack as well, and share these reasons with them. We invent more reasons.

Most people who see bears do so in zoological gardens. In a given year in the U.S., more people visit zoos than attend all sports events combined. When I heard this piece of information, a picture formed in my mind, of small children dragging parents out the door with pleas to go to the zoo. We went there last week, Mom says. That was a whole week ago, the children say.

They want to see the bears.

Most zoo bears are neurotics, cut off from habitat, traditions, and lifeways. Our estrangement from our native habitat has knocked us similarly off kilter. Our entwined history with bears continues.

While dismissing the idea that we share emotions with animals—a symptom of our self-imposed neurosis—we allow bears in captivity to experience some of ours: boredom, suffering, and trivialization. Kids throw things at them and try to poke them with sticks. While many zoos now serve as vital breeding grounds for species facing extinction, and many have been redesigned to allow the inmates more freedom, I cannot shake my childhood image of bears in circuses and zoos, imprisoned for our entertainment.

From there it is a short step to the claim that animals lack emotions and don't feel pain.

From there is it short step to believing that animals don't deserve our respect or a modicum of courtesy.

From there it is a tiny hop to the tourist in Yellowstone who rolled down his car window in June to slap a bear on the hindquarters.

A Heart in the Shape of a Bear

Why does the grizzly bear mother who wears radio collar number 399 bring her cubs out of the wilderness and close to a busy highway in Grand Teton National Park? Some have suggested it is to protect her cubs from larger bears who might harm them if not for the hundreds of photographers perched on car roofs nearby.

Perhaps her proximity to the roadside has been less intentional than circumstantial. She gives birth to her cubs in the remote Teton Wilderness and when they are ready to travel she introduces them to the various food sources within her large home range. At a certain time in spring, part of her domain includes abundant fields of Wyeth biscuitroot. On those gravel flats near Pilgrim Creek where the wildflowers grow, and beside the shadowed coverts of Willow Flats and Oxbow Bend where elk calves lie in hiding, food is plentiful.

In this part of her home range there happens to be a roadway. She tolerates us while showing her young what is good to eat. When the biscuitroot goes to seed and the elk move into the mountains, so does she.

After the death of her little white-faced cub, a temporary memorial was placed at the site by mourners. Made from river rocks and glacier-deposited cobbles, it lies on the shoulder of the highway, a heart with round appendages for bear ears. Someday, after the mother bear's inevitable death, the Park Service will likely construct a paved pullout with a plaque commemorating the famous bear, known for her longevity, productivity, and for what a fine parent she was.

Like Scarface in Yellowstone, the beloved bear who never caused a problem for his many years until he was shot by a hunter in the fall of 2015, the bear we call 399 will follow her cub Snowy into oblivion. Frost heaves and elk hooves will scatter the heart-shaped stones. All of us who remember this bear and her offspring will follow into the land of the dead. Perhaps there we will be reunited with our kin. Perhaps, at last, we will recognize them.

A Change of Heart

After the stones are scattered, after the photos on the plaque have faded and its surface is crazed by exposure to the Wyoming sun, after we have passed into the kingdom of the dead, what ripple of grace will we leave on the still and silent pool of our passing?

Maybe nothing more than this: with our stories and photographs, we will share our gratitude that one bear was able to impart such insight into her secret, private life. She showed us the depths to which we can feel affection for creatures other than ourselves. She showed us how she loved her cubs, played with them, taught them. She shared with us her beauty and intelligence. Through her, we were reconnected with the wild world from which we as a culture have detached. Seeing her, we remembered the experience of wonder.

What can we give her in return? How can we make amends for having betrayed her with our roads and cars and imperial lifeways? We can pass on what she shared with us to those who did not see, like elders around a campfire.

We will silence the restless young ones, wait for the latecomers to take their seats. We will pause before speaking to invoke the spirits residing in the treetops, mountaintops, and stars. Then we will lay another log on the flame and commence to tell our story.

Land and Bones
Susan Austin

Wind roars home after a windless winter. I listen to its long-haul howl, wonder how spring birds weather a force that tips thin-rooted aspen, rattles windows and doors in their jams, as if the wind was an intruder, or someone lost, or someone lonely.

For a time I lived in a homestead cabin built by two brothers from St. Joe: craftsmen, bakers, one a fiddler who snowshoed four miles to play music at the dance hall Saturday nights. My closest neighbor lived three miles down an unplowed road, wind a more common presence than stillness. Ferocious blizzards, blinding blizzards spun me around more than once on the long trek home.

The brothers built the fourteen by twenty-eight cabin in 1910. The logs they hewed by hand. No family here to tell their stories. The last old-timer who knew the brothers talked about courting in the heart of winter on a horse-drawn sleigh. She sang, *Sleigh bells ring, are you listening?* She said lips were too cold to form a kiss.

My husband's mother tells a story of winter not so far from here. She comes from Dakota pioneers. In the winter of 1922, in Bathgate, North Dakota, her mother, Mary Jane McAulay, went next door to a ladies' party. An aimless flurry became an almighty blizzard. Francis McAulay went out in the storm to help his Mary Jane home, leaving their three small children behind. He did not know that Mary Jane was already on her way, guided by the fence that separated the two houses. Francis floundered for hours as snow drifted in his path.

Lost to the fence, to his house, to Mary Jane, Francis vowed if he ever made it back home and found his family safe they would not spend another winter in North Dakota. The following year, before the days turned cold, Francis moved his family to Kelso, Washington.

The brothers carved a field and hewed a cabin and did not ask for much more. They came from Missouri as tie hacks and cleared the land with axes and crosscut saws. I imagine them with their backs bent to the sun pulling weeds by hand. One brother walked to town on snowshoes crafted from chokecherry stems, a fiddle slung over his shoulder. Summer afternoons, neighbors drove their wagons up the rough road for a slice of fresh baked bread. I'm told they grew the sweetest carrots around.

When their Missouri sisters sent word they would be arriving soon by train, the brothers hurried to hang the white lace curtains their sisters had sewn.

When you have lived in a place for a long time, so long you know it breathes, the land begins to whisper its secrets to you.

Fonnie Jones left a bucket of pink sponge curlers and a broom full of hair in a Winston-Salem beauty shop, Harry Jones come all the way east to fetch her after the war. They lived in a white house beside the creek, whistling willows, snow half a window high.

Fonnie wrote, *25 below and snowing.* She wrote, *Wind.* She wrote, *Cold.* She wrote, *The pickup is stuck in the snow.* April 17 she wrote, *The sandhill cranes have come home.*

A cloak of fog disguised the homestead when my husband walked into the milky air and stumbled on a weathered wood and coal-forged farm drill. The rest he imagined. He woke in the morning, late summer grass shedding night's frost. *I'll stay,* he said. He hung his backpack on the wall and called it home.

I skied blind through a night blizzard, at times down on my hands and knees searching for a remnant of a track. Lost and knowing it, I skied into white. Then I felt what seemed like a tap on my shoulder; a gust of cold wind shoved me backward. I turned just in time to see the gold glow of a kerosene lamp in a window, the silhouette of a man waiting. I hung my backpack on the wall beside his and called it home.

Fonnie said, *Weather has all the say. Learn to love white. Touch wood.* Vocabulary: freezing rain, fog, soup, hail, graupel, rime, whiteout, powder, sugar, champagne, hoarfrost, mashed potatoes, cement, rot, corn, ice, sun cup, breakable sun fuck, rain.

The story upwind was that Judd shot a raven from his pickup. Shot the bird in the wing so he could watch it suffer as it fell.

One summer morning, Judd sprayed the cabin with 2,4-D.

It was the time of year when my eyes surfed barley corduroyed by wind, real enough for me to lose my longing for the sea. It was the time of year when purple thistle flowers dotted fields, creek sides, lots parceled out for sale. It was the time of year I felt nervous when I heard a low-flying plane.

I was still wrapped in dreams when Judd crested the hill in his crop duster. He took a disliking to move-ins. My husband ran barefoot into the barley field just beyond the cabin. He waved his arms over his head to let Judd know we were home. We shoved towels around the old window frames, small four pane windows, low enough that I imagined the brothers stooping to watch snow climb the cabin walls, or to watch the cow moose with her calf that wintered nearby, or the barley burn in the sun, or the barley ripped clean through by hail; windows that let wind do its talking, inviting dirt from the fields inside.

I stood in the center of the cabin, my eyes still dull with sleep, and listened as the plane dove, leveled off, and dumped 2,4-D on the roof. Judd flew two low passes with the nozzles open. The 2,4-D rained down on the tin roof and rested like dew on the pink crane's bill blooming in the front yard. The 2,4-D drifted in.

The extension agent said he'd nearly bathed himself in the stuff hundreds of times. Sprayed it by hand on his own fields. He said, "The worst it's done is blistered my arms."

Two days went by. I watched the thistle twist on itself, the wildflowers in the yard.

I tried to teach the dog not to sleep where I shoveled snow to melt for water, and then I gave in. The drift that formed was a natural shelter for her. Through blinding blizzards, she led me home. And when the world became maddening white, the same white that drove some prairie women crazy, that brown dog would sit in that patch of snow I used for making water, the only thing not white as far as my eyes could see.

I wrote words in the snow that a stranger might read before the wind caught me talking to a mountain and erased the slate. Too long left to myself, words fell apart from their meaning.

"By God no!" the brothers said when the rural co-op brought electricity to the valley.

How many days did the brothers stare out the windows, snow burying the north wall to the eaves, iron pop of the wood stove?

The sound of 2,4-D raining on a tin roof sounds like a summer squall, like hail burst through a thunderhead.

The blue-black ravens heckle. Quick wit of the wind. I run into the field, bare legs slashed by barley stalks. A hard rain bites my face. I picture Judd in his crop duster, lift a rifle to my shoulder and aim. I shoot for the wings so Judd will suffer as he falls.

I like to believe that only the weather can change the cabin, wear it to dust by wind and rain and snow. First the brittle chinking falls out in places and the wind bores wider holes. Snow drifts inside; rain seeps and blows through. The cabin becomes a marmot house, with straw and fuzz from our winter hats matted in mouse nests. The foundation settles too much in a fast spring melt and the cabin leans north, then topples in the wind. Bare bones bleached and scattered, like the cow moose who lay down in the aspen grove, leaving her calf to fend off coyotes just two weeks before the snow eased. The calf was smart to leave the rot of its mother. Coyotes and ravens and one bald eagle finished her off, scattered the bones.

One winter night I drove to the end of the plowed road and parked next to the granary, two-by-fours stacked and lapped at the corners. I thought I would curl on the truck seat and sleep awhile but the cold quickly chilled my bones. I lifted my pack to my back and began the three mile ski home.

Under a new moon, dense fog meeting snow, I skied into colder air that settles in the creek bottom. The sharp corner of the dugway reminded me of the etched curve of my husband's hip. Instead of hurrying to warm covers, I lingered. The scent of a moose lingered too in the still air. Coyotes sang. When the coyotes quieted, I heard the faint hoot of a great horned owl.

Across the upper field I wandered off track, circled the chicken coop and the shed. Finally I reached out into the fog and touched the sawdust-and-splinter-chink, the hand-hewn logs of the cabin. I felt what the brothers must have known—the dips and contours and flat reaches, with no other guidance than the land in their bones.

Across a white field a seam of mending. Two wolves, or snowshoe tracks leading home.

Sections of this manuscript were previously published in different form in Leaning Into The Wind, Mariner Books, 1998; Woven on the Wind, Mariner Books, 2002, and Northern Lights.

2,4-D is an herbicide categorized as an endocrine-disrupting chemical, and myriad laboratory studies have demonstrated a link between human thyroid disorders and 2,4-D. The International Agency for Research on Cancer declared 2,4-D a possible human carcinogen in 2015, based on research demonstrating that it causes cancer in laboratory animals and damages human cells.
https://www.nrdc.org/stories/24-d-most-dangerous-pesticide-youve-never-heard

Garter Snakes on the Dike
Stephen S. Lottridge

A woman was jogging down a trail in South Africa. She was wearing a green tank top and matching shorts. Her brown running shoes blended with the color of the earth. Her amber hair swayed in a ponytail as she moved. The early morning air was sweet and cool. Her stride was easy, unhurried; her breathing was steady and deep. Birds sang. The world seemed at ease. Serene. Edenic.

Suddenly, she broke stride, stopped, froze, without knowing why. She was alert, anxious, confused, urgently aware of "something," some danger. Silent, she scanned the ground. Then, she saw the cobra, beside the trail ahead, just out of striking range. She stood immobile, her heart thudding. Stationary. Waiting. Gradually, with time, the snake wove off into the bush. She backed up slowly, glancing behind her and then forward again. The snake did not reappear. She turned, still vigilant, and walked gingerly away.

National Public Radio told this story to illustrate the fact that we primates have developed, over millennia, a special visual sensitivity to the presence of reptiles, especially snakes. According to research, we can be alerted to the proximity of a snake, can somehow "see" it, before our eyes consciously make it out. Other senses, such as smell and hearing, may originally have been implicated, but sight has become primary as we primates have evolved. This subtle acuity has been crucial to the survival of our species. We may not be consciously aware of it, just as we may not be overtly receptive to many of the delicate communications our senses register. We may be too engrossed in the concerns of our daily lives to mark and attend to these messages. But this subliminal signal is always there, whether we heed it or not.

One of the boons of living in Teton County, Wyoming, is that no poisonous snakes are native here. There are certainly dangers. Grizzly bears have extended their range from the north, rendering encounters more frequent. Even a native black bear may turn rogue. Mountain lions pose a risk now and again. Coyotes may savage your untended dog. But there are no poisonous snakes. A few residents may keep such reptiles as pets, but none exist in the wild. Yet. Climate change may bring rattlers up from the Green. But for now, there are none.

What we do have are small, beautiful garter snakes. Big ones run maybe a foot and a half or two feet long. I met one once, up Game Creek, who may even have been pushing a yard. Mostly, though, they cap out at something around fifteen or eighteen inches. So they're not that big, as snakes go. They often have a warm orange stripe on their backs, and robin's egg blue underbellies, the rest of their bodies being mostly light to medium brown. Their tongues are flashing ribbons of reddish lace, mobile and quick. Their eyes are a facetted black. The best place to see them, although they are everywhere, is on the dike along the Snake River. They live and breed in the rocks on the sides of the dike, and down on the overgrown river bed where the water no longer flows. They frequently come up onto the top of the dike, to catch the sun and warm themselves, I suppose. Whyever they come, come they do, and lie there on the gritty flats. And that is where I often happen upon them.

Garter snakes in Wyoming differ vastly from the Cape cobra, of course. Even so, I often have what is, evidently, a typical, primate survival response when walking on the dike. I will have a sudden awareness—not conscious, really, more of a visceral sensation—of "something there." I may shy slightly, and become inadvertently and intensely alert. I scan the ground. And then, and only then, do I consciously see the snake. Sometimes it is just sunning itself on the warmed earth. Most often, though, it is moving, working its way toward the side of the dike, disturbed, perhaps, by my footfalls or the dog's ranging. Maybe it is just on its own way, for its own reasons.

I always stop to look, and feel a certain quiver in my body. I don't experience fear, exactly, although that is probably at the root of it. It is more like intense focus. I don't really know how to read snakes. A coiled rattlesnake, head up, rattle aquiver, I can read. And one just gliding along on its own business, that, too, I can read and let pass. But mostly not. Not the way I can read dogs, or even cats, sometimes. So I focus, although on what, I am not entirely sure. Just focus for its own, and evidently my ancient survival's, sake.

I have actually come to feel quite friendly toward these little snakes. I am sure I would feel very different if they were cobras. But they are not. They do have a mild toxin in their saliva, but they are not a danger to humans. They do not usually act aggressively, although I did see a tiny one dart a quick little stab of a strike once, when my younger daughter tried to poke her finger at its head. On the other hand, they don't seem particularly shy. They just act like themselves, part of the world we share.

I don't know if that daughter of mine feels the same mildly anxious alertness that I do. She denied it when I asked her once, but then, she is not excessively introspective. Whether she feels fear or not, she has proven herself eager to engage the snakes full on, to share the world with them physically and close up. If we see one, she darts after it and tries to pick it up. They are far charier of contact than she and try frantically to wiggle away. If she does manage to catch one, which she often does, she picks it up and holds it and examines it and lets it twine over her hands and arms.

Once, I left her in the care of a friend who had a son about her age. It was a rural area with lots of rocks and grass and ponds. When I came to pick her up, she was beside herself with excitement. She dragged me to one of the ponds, where a handful of other children were gathered. She pulled me over to a small, red and white cooler on the bank. Exclaiming "Look, Dad, look, see what I got," she bent over, her frilly pink dress aflutter in the breeze as she opened the cooler, plunged her right hand inside and pulled out a great cluster of garter snakes. They were small, about a foot long, so she could clutch a bountiful bunch, even with her small hand. They writhed and twisted as she gleefully held them out toward me, Medusa's head on the end of her arm.

My reaction was mixed, as you might imagine. I admired her *sang-froid* and delighted in her joy and enthusiasm. I also felt nervous and protective. I hid my uncertainty as best I could and joined in with her exhilaration and sense of accomplishment. She kept telling me that there were hundreds of them there and how she had caught more than anybody. As she went to put them back in the cooler, one escaped. Holding the remaining ones aloft in her right hand, she hopped over in her patent leather shoes and white socks and deftly caught the escapee with her left. She skillfully returned them all to the cooler, closing it carefully as she stuffed heads and tails back inside. She took pains not to hurt them. They were not only her captives; they were also her pets and playmates.

In some small way, I adopt her approach to the snakes as mine when I walk on the dike. I experience myself as a brother to them, albeit a leery one. Sometimes I talk to them. I suppose, initially, I speak to ease my own primitive anxiety. Primate, reptile, uh-oh. By talking to them, I reassure myself of my own safety. I suppose I would offer to shake hands if they could, to show that I mean them no harm and to be persuaded of their good intentions. I haven't tried getting down and wriggling beside one as a way of peacefully joining it, though that bizarre idea has occurred to me. I comment on the weather and temperature, knowing that those things matters to them. I mention how glad I am to see them, and compliment them on their beauty and grace. I often exclaim delightedly. I speak to calm them if they seem startled or in unnecessary haste or agitation. I admire their litheness and agility, and tell them that I find the way they move over, around and under impediments impressive. I am sweetly drawn to the flicking of their filigree tongues as I lean over them. And more and more often these days, I urge them off the dike.

The dike this summer has become a place of reptile carnage. Gravel trucks ply the road that tops the dike. They used to appear seldom; now they pass frequently. Evidently, it has been decided—by whom, I do not know—that the banks containing and channeling the river need to be repaired. I can only guess why. I have not noticed any damage. But whatever the reasons, work has proceeded apace. Most, if not all, of the work has been taking place on the west bank dikes, and that has involved heavy truck traffic on both sides of the river, up and downstream from the highway on the west side and, most noticeably, on the east side up from Emily's Pond to the rock quarry and back. Sometimes the trucks carry gravel; as often they carry rip rap. Whatever they carry, and even when they are running void, they are giant, loud, pounding machines.

These trucks squash the garter snakes. Have you ever seen a garter snake run over by a gravel truck loaded with rip rap? I don't mean one that has been run over; I mean one that is being run over. The snake wriggles as it feels the truck approach. It moves this way and that. But the sound in the air and the trembling in the ground are too general and confusing. It can't reckon which direction the danger is coming from so it can't figure out which way promises escape. It freezes, madly flicking its tongue. And the truck comes on. The giant tires, maybe five feet in diameter and a foot and a half wide, pound down the dirt. In the last instant, as the snake starts to dart aside, the tread catches its tail and rolls up the body. Blood and innards spurt and splash, a quick death thrash, the skull pops. The tire leaves a dark patch for the next couple of rotations until the blood and matter are dispersed and absorbed. A reddish-black ribbon lies in the road, with a faint yellow line and twisted, robin's egg blue stripe where the snake flipped at the last instant. That is all that remains. That and my primate heightened awareness still. But now there are two dangers. The primordial fear of the snake, even dead, and the modern, conscious fear of the machine that killed it, and could kill me.

I identify with the snake. I imagine the truck coming after me. I imagine running, stopping, turning, turning back, not entirely sure where the danger is. I feel the bump of the grille, the tires catching the bottoms of my toes, rolling up the soles of my feet as I fall, the blood and flesh splattering out under both sides of the tire as it crushes my legs, thighs, buttocks, torso, my guts spewing out my mouth and nose, my eyes exploding from their sockets and my skull popping dully as it is crushed.

One second of perplexing, exquisite agony, maybe two, and done. The truck rolls on, painting a few red stripes in the gravel, fainter with each rotation of the wheel, leaving a mess of cloth and senseless matter behind it, the rip rap thumping in its bed, going to hold the river in its place.

I know the driver would try to stop for me, if he saw me. At least, I believe that. I know it is my own morbid imagination that creates this gruesome fantasy. The image lies in my mind alone, my own waking nightmare. And yet . . . . I tell myself that I wave to the truck drivers in comradeship, and that is true. I respect and benefit from their work. I also wave to placate them, and to assuage my own anxiety, for I am afraid of the trucks. My body tenses and I feel apprehension when I hear their roar in the distance. I stand nervously at the extreme edge of the road, holding my trembling dog by her collar. My nightmarish image of my own death aside, my body is truly frail and vulnerable in relation to the trucks. If one veered, I would, in fact, be crushed.

If my dog darted out—she has no more sense of vehicles than do the snakes—she would become as confused as they and would be killed. I know this depends on the drivers, mostly. But, from my perspective, soft, vulnerable and slow as I am on the roadway, the drivers, high and anonymous in the cab, are part of the truck, which I fear far more than I do the snakes. Their danger is real; that of the snakes is ancestral and unreal in the present.

The snakes are my brothers and sisters, my family. We have evolved together, if warily. We both feel pain, I believe. We are both drawn to the warmth of the sun, and born of it. We both make our ways along the dike. I am cautious of them, vigilant. And they of me. Yet when they die, some part of me dies with them. When they are run over, I feel the hard, hot, nubbled tread on my skin. I am anciently afraid of them, yet they are kin and some part of my family in this world is lost when they are killed.

We humans are all complicit in such slaughter. I am directly complicit. When I go to the dike, I drive a vehicle from my house to the parking area, destroying who knows how many creatures I do not even notice. I try to be careful, but I am not always attentive or aware. In the past, I have actually been aware but uncaring. Once, as a young man, driving down out of the Sierras on a scorching summer's day in an old VW, years before the interstate and air conditioning in cars, I came around a curve, fast. I was tired, sweaty, irritated, leading a life I could not figure out how to escape. A rattlesnake was in my lane, just ahead, crossing the road. Not fast, not slow, just crossing. I could have stood on the brakes or maybe even swerved into the other lane. I am not sure to this day why I didn't. There may have been oncoming traffic, but I think not.

Over the years that I have told this story, in my own justification I have said there was, but as I look at the image of that moment in my mind now, the oncoming lane is clear. I no longer remember the truth for certain. What I do remember is hitting the snake smack in the middle of its body, at speed. It was not a big snake, some two and a half or three feet long, chunky. I saw the rattles clearly, stuck up at an angle the way rattlers hold them when they move. And through the open window, through the blanket of wind in my ears, I heard the searing hiss of its rattles, like the sound of a steam press in an old cleaners, as my right front tire smashed into and through its midsection.

In the rearview mirror I saw it thrash and flip and lie still. At the time, I felt triumphant. It was a rattler, after all. It could have killed me. But the fact is, it was doing me no harm. Just on its way to somewhere, moving along for its own reasons. I regret that moment to this day, but I cannot deny it. And I've killed other creatures for no good reason, on purpose or by accident, or somewhere in between. I know I am not alone in this. All of us share responsibility for such damage, to one degree or another. But I am most responsible for myself.

If I am directly implicated, I participate indirectly, as well. I come specifically to walk on the dike built by men and trucks like the ones that are splattering the snakes. I enjoy that walking. It provides me with exercise and natural beauty on all sides. I take pleasure in it and am grateful for it. I wave to the truck drivers as they pull past, for whatever complex of motives. They almost always wave back. I have even come to recognize some of them, and perhaps they me.

At times, I do wonder what the valley would be like without all this diking and ordering; if the river ran free. But I do nothing to advocate for that, nor do I even believe I would wish it to be true, except in theory. I would probably not even be able to live here in this place I love if that were the case. So I am a participant, passively, in the building and maintenance of the dike and all that entails.

Something larger is at play here. We built the dike to contain the river. Much of Jackson Hole is a flood plain. The river used to braid its way throughout the valley, weaving this way and that from year to year. Rather than accommodate ourselves to the river, however, and live where it did not flood or flow, we humans redirected the river to suit our desires. We diked it and leveed it and dredged it and channeled it so it would flow where we wanted it to. That alteration allowed us to build houses and other structures, to cultivate ranch land, pasture cattle and lay roads, to create communities, to do the things we desired; to tame the wild. Oh, we left room for the water to flow, but strictly within the confines we had constructed.

As a species, we are engineers. As much as anything else, perhaps more than anything else, we alter our environment. We want to have an effect on our surroundings. It is not merely a matter of control, although it is that. More deeply, it is the desire to make an impact, to leave a mark. Because we have become so proficient at devising tools, such as the trucks, we are much more effective at leaving our mark than are other beings. Our ability to change the consistency of natural materials lets us redesign our environment more lastingly that do other creatures. There is no inherent value, either positive or negative, in this capability. It is just there, neutral.

The same impulse that leads us to alter the river and restrict the water's freedom leads us to construct the world's great buildings and monuments. The impulse to give a different form to our material surroundings has created some of the world's most beautiful art as well as its most hideous excrescences. Construction and destruction come from the same urge.

I ponder the source of this desire. Probably the combination of opposable thumbs, language and a large forebrain contribute to it. Our conceptions of time and of self must centrally direct our desire to leave our imprint on the world we inhabit. We can see the future and know our lives will end. Leaving our mark may seem to be a way to counter our death. Whatever the true motivation, we justify our activity with our comfort, our safety, our convenience, our beliefs. Often, we conflate our desires with needs and claim necessity as justification. And as often, we do not count the collateral damage. We do not even see it, or, if we do, we do not take it into our reckoning. We do not count the cost of our actions to the beings that share our earth, and in that discounting we harm ourselves as well.

I say that is who we are as a species. At the same time, many of us have countervailing intentions. We try to be as unobtrusive in our environment as we can, especially out in the wilderness that surrounds us. Leave no trace. Pack it in; pack it out. Even in town: recycle, walk if you can, reduce your carbon footprint. Stand silently to watch the sun rise or set. Rue even the contrails that mark the high air, the artificial satellites passing across the night sky, the light pollution that dims our view of the universe.

The desire to fit seamlessly into our environment, to stand in awe of it, to be an integral part of the rest of nature, exists in us. That desire is just much less developed in our culture, and perhaps in our very nature, than is the urge to alter our environment for our own purposes.

I think there is no way around this issue. We create, we destroy. We erect, we take down. But we must realize that every action has consequences. Every change we make, no matter how we intend it and no matter what benefits it brings to us, and even to other creatures, brings loss with it. There is always a cost. No part of a system can change without affecting everything else in the system, to the greatest or slightest degree. And we are all part of one system, whether we want to acknowledge that or not.

I sorrow for the garter snakes. They are collateral damage in the construction work of our engineering species. We want to constrain the river. We sacrifice the snakes in our endeavor. Perhaps there is nothing we can do about that. We cannot stop being who we are. But we need not condemn ourselves to blunder heedlessly through our lives, ignoring the consequences, even unintended, of our actions. I do not believe that collateral damage ought just to be written off. At the very least, we must acknowledge it and embrace all the emotions our awareness evokes.

So... I walk on the dike. I wave to the truck drivers. I continue to be glad there is a dike to walk on, with entrancing views of the river and mountains. I am blessed by the presence of eagles and ospreys and trumpeter swans, whose companionship I might not otherwise enjoy so closely. I am glad I have a house that is not flooded, and a car to transport my old body to the dike. As I walk, I practice what equanimity I can in the roar of the trucks' passing. I start at the presence of the garter snakes. I greet them and these days I try to shoo them off the top of the dike as the trucks bear down. I sorrow for their death when I fail, knowing that I am complicit in the very carnage I grieve.

What I Didn't Know About Hunting
Marcia Hensley

When I first moved from a city in the Midwest to small-town Rock Springs, Wyoming, I wondered why so many people drove pickup trucks with gun racks in the back windows. That fall, I learned it was because so many of them were hunters. Town would seem deserted on fall weekends, and stores would run special sales for "hunting widows" left behind while husbands, armed with hunting rifles, roamed the miles and miles of public lands in the region.

Hunting was a significant ritual in the town and surrounding communities. Gradually, I learned about what was, to me, a unique custom. Hunting seasons opened on various dates depending on what animal you wanted to hunt. One of the earliest seasons was for sage grouse (sage chickens, as locals call them), then came antelope, then seasons for deer and elk and moose, depending on whether you were bow hunting or hunting with a gun. Hunters had studied the dates and locations during the spring and summer, then sent in their applications to the Wyoming Game and Fish Department, who then determined by lottery who would hunt and where. Hunters might say, "I drew area 15," and hunters would know exactly where that was and had probably scouted it out before hunting season to learn details of the landscape and where the animals liked to hang out. I learned this from listening to colleagues on campus talk of their fall weekend plans. Hunting wasn't just a "guy thing" here in Wyoming. Some of my women colleagues were just as experienced as the men.

One vividly bright, very windy September morning, I got my first taste of Wyoming hunting culture. Not that I carried a gun. I'd never used one and didn't want to start. But I tagged along with my new husband, Mike, on a sage chicken hunt. This hunt was on private property, a neighbor's ranch. We gathered for coffee at the ranch house, then spread out to walk different fields where we might flush out sage chickens. The hay had been cut, baled, and stacked, leaving golden fields park-like and open. The sage chickens hung out in the remaining tall grasses along the irrigation ditches, and wandered into the sagebrush of unfarmed sections.

They would fly up out of their cover as we got near them, and Mike would take aim and shoot. Sage chickens don't fly very high, but they're quick and it's an adrenaline rush to see several of them suddenly burst out of their cover, into the air before your eyes.

Although the sun was warm, the wind was blowing hard out of the northwest, keeping us cool—a typical fall day in Wyoming. We stalked sage chicken all morning, and Mike shot a few. I carried their limp, plump bodies by the feet, admiring the herringbone pattern of their feathers, light brown, grey, and white, still vibrant in the sun.

When Mike and I returned to the ranch house, we found that some of the other hunters' sage chickens were already cleaned and soaking in salt water to minimize their wild flavor. Then, they were fried in egg and flour batter, just like southern fried chicken. "Good eating," most everyone agreed. Eating the meat that had been harvested, I came to understand, was a point of honor among hunters. Although they enjoyed the sport of hunting, sport wasn't all that mattered.

Years later, when collecting stories for a history of the area, I learned that sage chicken was a staple in the diet of early settlers. One old-timer told how when she was pregnant, she was craving the taste of sage chicken, but it wasn't hunting season. Her obliging husband shot a few anyway and brought them home, where she cooked them up on the spot. Unexpectedly, a Fish and Game warden they knew dropped by to say hello. They spoke casually about the nice day, and, since dinner was nearly ready, invited the warden to join them. He complimented the nervous woman on a delicious dinner, and went on his way without a mention of what he surely realized was an infraction, leaving the family greatly relieved and grateful.

Sheltered from the formidable wind in our host's garage, we present-day hunters watched the chicken sizzle in a huge cast-iron skillet, drank beer or soda, and swapped stories, not only of the day's hunting experience, but also of past sage chicken hunts. Our day culminated when we sat down at picnic tables to eat our harvest, along with potato salad, corn on the cob, and an assortment of desserts. A dinner party—Wyoming style!

Some of the social qualities of the sage chicken dinner party carried over into big game hunting; however, hunting big game was a much more serious undertaking, requiring a great deal of planning, gathering of supplies, and plotting of strategies in endless conversations with hunting buddies. It started with making the decision of what area to hunt in, coordinating applications to Game and Fish, and then waiting to find out the results. As the opening date grew closer, the talk became more intense. Tents, sleeping bags, cots, and guns were dragged out of storage, examined and cleaned as needed. Scouting trips were made. Some hunters would even hire a small private plane and its pilot to fly low over the mountain areas to see where the elk herds were gathering.

Once, Mike and his buddies hunted near the elk feeding ground near Pinedale, where elk would be given hay when the deep snows limited natural forage. After it snowed during the night, the guys woke to find dozens of elk bedded down around their tents. Unfortunately for the hunters, they had left their guns in the trucks, so not one of the elk was shot that day. The hunters loved to tell this story on themselves, and were obviously satisfied with the thrill of being surrounded by the beautiful animals.

The major hunt for Mike and his buddies was for elk in the Wind River Mountains, about 40 miles north of our home. The hunting buddies, Jim, Jerry, Billy, and Mike, colleagues teaching at the community college in Rock Springs, had a favorite spot to hunt elk. They returned every year for about ten years to Lamaroux Meadow, near Big Sandy Openings. To get there, they drove about 40 miles from our place in Farson, gradually ascending into the mountains through the desert over gravel and dirt roads with bone-rattling washboard surfaces. After crossing a bridge over the Big Sandy River, and winding through lodge pole forest, they would come out into a great, open meadow. On the other side was a knoll sheltered by pines, with a view of the meadow and mountain peaks. This knoll was where the men would pitch their tents. But getting across the meadow could be tricky, since it barely had a two-track road and it often had deep mud and standing water. Sometimes the guys with the bigger trucks would have to tow in the less powerful vehicles, like Whitey, our 1963 Jeep, or later, our 1980 Chevy pickup, Old Blue.

Labor Day was the date designated for setting up the tents, which would then be left in place until the end of hunting season or the first major snow, whichever came first. The hunting buddies would set up camp, go back to teach their classes during the week, and leave as early as possible on Friday afternoon to return to camp. I was always amazed that although they left all their camping equipment inside the tents, they never had anything stolen or damaged. The meadow's remoteness was its protection.

The Labor Day camp was special because wives and girlfriends were invited. Sometimes, Labor Day coincided with the first cold rains or snows of the season. Like the time Mike, Jim, and I arrived in a downpour, after sloshing and sliding over muddy roads all the way in. Since Jim's tent was already up, and pitching ours would have been nearly impossible in the cold, hard rain, we all huddled in one tent, trying to keep warm and dry. If it had just been the three of us, it wouldn't have been too bad, but each of us had a dog with us, and Jim had picked up a stray he'd found wandering along the forest road. I spent a long, sleepless night breathing the odor of wet dogs, listening to the wind howling and rain drumming against the tent canvas. Would one of those trees topple over on us? Would the tent begin to leak? Was that a dog or one of the guys snoring?

But usually, the weather would be crisp and sunny on Labor Day, and we womenfolk enjoyed the beautiful days and camaraderie, experiencing some of the adventure of hunting camp. You might think the women would be expected to do the cooking, but this wasn't the case. The men prided themselves on planning and cooking sumptuous campfire meals.

Naturally, they would bring steaks and potatoes, but also would bring sausages, shrimp, or even lobster tails. Many ice chests filled with food, beer, and pop were required for this hunting camp. Everyone pooled their contributions for a giant campfire cookout potluck. The party extended late into the night while we watched stars emerge over the meadow, and then listened to coyotes and owls serenade us. We imagined bears lurking in forest shadows where we went, guided by flashlight beams, when we needed to relieve ourselves. We thought we heard wolves howling, and de-bated whether the Yellowstone wolves, introduced a decade earlier, could have migrated down into the Wind River Range by now. It seemed likely.

The hunters rose before dawn and ventured out in the cold, while the rest of us snuggled in sleeping bags. When they returned mid-morning, they cooked a big breakfast of eggs, bacon, hash browns, and sausage to sustain us until dinner. If the hunters had been successful, they had to re-turn to haul the carcass back. Preferably, if it was in an accessible spot, they could return in to camp on Jim's four-wheeler. Otherwise, they'd have to cut it up and pack it out. Finding where they'd left their kill and reaching it before a coyote, mountain lion, or bear did wasn't easy, but they knew the country well and would have marked the trail. They had given names to certain features of the landscape to orient themselves. There was Stacy's Meadow, named after Jim's daughter, Marcia's Marsh, named for me, the aptly-named Struggle-Up Hill, and numerous other personal landmarks.

While the hunters worked, the rest of us sat in folding chairs in the shade if the day was warm, or around the campfire if it was cold, dis-cussing college politics, sharing family concerns, or exploring whatever topics came up. The guys played horseshoes, drank too much beer, and reminisced about past hunting adventures. Sometimes, Mike and I hiked over to the river to fly fish in the late afternoon while the hunters who were unsuccessful in the morning might go out again to try their luck. We didn't start cooking dinner until dark, when they returned. The simple, unhurried routine was an antidote to our often stressful professional lives.

Labor Day hunting camp at Lamaroux Meadow was a highlight of our year, marking the end of summer and ushering in fall. After that weekend, only the dedicated hunters went up to camp and the serious hunting began. Just before dark on a Sunday evening during this season, I'd look for a pickup to arrive. There'd be a tired, filthy, happy Mike, and sometimes, protruding from the pickup bed, the antlers or legs of an unlucky elk. The animal would have to be strung up by its hind legs in the garage and allowed to bleed out before being skinned and prepared for freezing. Sometimes Mike would take his animal to a professional meat market for processing, instead of doing it himself.

After those weekends, Mike might not return with his elk, but he always had harrowing or funny stories of what happened at hunting camp—who had been successful, details of the animals harvested, and how difficult the hunt had been. One of the legendary stories was the time Jim stood too close to the campfire and set his jeans ablaze. Another was when the guys were playing poker in the tent with a propane stove for heat. The tent caught fire and when Billy suggested they should try to put it out, Jim said, "Not until you play your hand." The lore of hunting camp at Lamaroux Meadow grew with the years and created a strong bond between the hunters and their families.

Before being married to a hunter, I really hadn't thought much about why people hunt. I had been a city girl, and the men I knew spent their weekends watching football around a T.V. rather than bonding around a campfire in the wilderness. I came to understand that for Mike, his buddies, and the other hunters I came to know, hunting was a refuge. They entered the wilderness with an awareness of its rich history and complex ecology. They felt the presence of Native Americans who had hunted there before them; the mountain men who had trapped beaver there; the early settlers who felled the pines to build cabins in the meadows, eking out a living by hunting, fishing, and trapping.

They brought to their hunting experiences a story imbedded in the American character: a man alone in the wilderness, knowing it well, able to meet the challenges of surviving in it, feeling at one with it. Hunting wasn't just about killing animals, or providing meat for their families, or about drinking beer around a campfire. It was a way to relive those satisfying primal roles for themselves.

In the early 2000s, the Forest Service closed many of the roads leading into Wyoming wilderness areas. The road into Lamaroux Meadow was one of them. For a couple of years Mike and his hunting buddies tried driving their trucks as close to the meadow as they could and then ferrying tents, food and equipment over in four wheelers. Eventually Forest Service officials found out and sternly reprimanded them. We experimented with having Labor Day hunting camps at other spots in the Wind Rivers, but they never were as satisfying as the ones at Lamaroux Meadow. Then, a couple of the hunting buddies took jobs elsewhere, leaving only Jim and Mike. Thus, as with many good things, the legendary Labor Day hunting camp tradition came to an end, living on in the stories we told and retold around tamer campfires and in our memories of the camaraderie we shared around them. In hunting camp, surrounded by mountains, forests, streams wild creatures, and vast sky, we not only felt connected to each other, but also to our place in the natural world, and that helped us keep our lives in perspective.

Circle of Water
Tory Taylor

I stare straight up into the January sky of Yellowstone National Park. A perfect snowflake tumbles and spirals gently from lead-gray clouds and roosts softly on the wolf-fur ruff of my vintage down parka. I admire the flake for its delicate lines and angles. So fragile. So elegant. Scientists, for reasons similar to those of the Inuit and Chukchi peoples, have dozens of names for the many types of snow. The shape and structure of snowflakes and ice crystals are determined by such factors as air temperatures, humidity, and the atmospheric conditions in which they are formed. The perfect snowflake now perched on my parka is named stellar crystal, and was born in temperatures near the four degree Fahrenheit mark.

As I ponder this fine flake from heaven, it slowly melts into a tiny droplet of water as round and translucent as the eye of a sparrow. I shake my shoulders, throwing the droplet into an open section of the Lamar River. The droplet quietly plops into the serpentine stream like a small diamond into a fountain, and briefly creates a tiny ring. It is instantly swept downstream. My droplet has just completed one circle of its existence and immediately embarked on another. From the sky as perfect flake to parka as liquid sphere, the soujourning droplet blends with its own in the Lamar. There, the droplet joins a grand gathering of lemming-like droplets, gaining unstoppable strength in their push to the Yellowstone, the Missouri, the Mississippi.

From the cold current of the Lamar, no one knows the fate of my droplet. Perhaps someday it will again fall to earth in some parched desert, as precious as angel tears. Or perhaps it may appear again as stellar crystal on the Greenland ice cap, there to take its place in the layers upon hundreds of layers of snow compressed by weight and time. Only seventy to ninety percent of glacial ice is actually water; the rest is trapped air and gas locked fast in frozen time like an important document secured in a bank vault. This captive atmosphere may someday be freed by a curious scientist looking for clues of climates and conditions of ages long past. The layer of ice and trapped gas can be read like the layered pages of a book, telling us of ancient volcanoes, tropics, and ice ages.

I do not know the fate of my droplet with its restless bonds of hydrogen and oxygen. Will my gypsy jewel ever drop in again for a visit to Yellowstone? Like all things on earth, the water droplet is in constant motion, a divine dance with each and every participant swirling and swaying to its own rhythm. Rocks and snails do a slow waltz. Trees in the wind perform the twist. River rapids and chipmunks prefer a loud polka. Even the aged continents cannot help tapping their feet as the great dance floor of Earth revolves like an old 45 RPM record in a jukebox. Let the good times roll, and roll my dance-partner droplet to the sea!

To Hannah,
keep on writing!
Edit
Dec '16

Windy Acres
Edith Cook

It is spring 2016. I have moved into my home 50 miles north of where I used to live in Wyoming's capital. Smaller than my previous house, it was constructed on the homestead site that adjoins my defunct wheat farm. The acreage, including the contiguous state land, has lain fallow these past three years, reverting to grasses and wildflowers. I wonder if the state would set aside its parcel as natural habitat? Reviving my own 500 acres is a long shot, and I took risks building here; well, I was betting that Wyoming legislators would legalize agrarian hemp.

"This has got to be the windiest place in Wyoming," visitors comment as they arrive for my open house.

"As you can see, I've made good on my plans." I shake hands, smiling and greeting. "Welcome to my new abode! Mi casa su casa."

Yes, it's windy out here where my home hunkers down on the high plains. On the plus side, twelve years of living in Cheyenne accustomed my body to the altitude. No more, that pesky night time oxygen intake of my Wyoming beginnings. You *can* *t*each an old dog new tricks.

"So this is your former wheat field."

"Not all of it. The state of Wyoming owns 700 acres at the south end. The previous owner conveyed the state-land lease he held but continued to farm as sharecropper."

"And you've had the income for some years, right?"

"Long enough to pay off what I owed on the land. Together, the acreage used to yield a thousand to fifteen-hundred winter-wheat bushels per year."

To contain erosion, planting proceeded in strips on a rotational basis, leaving the previous year's strips fallow. Seed was planted in August, sprouted (with good luck and rain) in September, fell dormant through the winter, and returned to life in the spring. The cereal was harvested in July.

"Three years ago, the wheat sprouted poorly and came up stunted, yielding less than 400 bushels. Hail had destroyed the previous year's harvest. As you well know, ours is one of the driest states in the union—and today's weather instability renders rainfall even less dependable. My sharecropping farmer up and quit, citing climate-change problems."

What I don't mention: To cover land-lease obligations to the state, I had to borrow money from my youngest, a Silicon-Valley techie.

"Can you plant irrigated crops? Sugar beets? Corn?"

"We don't have the water for it. The wheat was raised in dry-land farming."

To keep myself from fretting about the impossible, I initiated container gardening, which I show off with pride. Raised-garden beds sprout spinach, lettuce, potatoes. Feed containers hold tomato plants, some already bearing small green fruit. Strawberries, geranium, and begonias round out my collection.

"The raised beds were meant to discourage wildlife, but this must have been a juvenile coyote." I point out dog-paw tracks that destroyed carrot seedlings in the outermost bed. "It couldn't have been Abby. She stays indoors at night."

I also show my friends the "living snow fences" in back of my house, three rows of inaugural trees. "The Resource District planted them in weed barriers and added a drip system. It's cost-shared, so it's affordable."

"My, but the trees are small," they tell me.

"I know it. They won't make any kind of barrier against wind and snow until years from now. But it's all I could get."

All the while Abby has been running around nuzzling guests, sniffing their crotches.

"You have an active dog," someone says.

"Well, she's still a teenager in human years. I am her forth owner. What traumas she's lived through I'll never know, but I pay attention to the signs. Like, needing to touch base with me often. She is in and out all day, scratching at the door, tracking snow and mud."

"A good-looking dog."

"Yes." Abby is Australian shepherd mix, short-haired, with the shepherd's dark grays and browns and the beautiful white "apron" of another breed.

"Yesterday I found her barking at an outside corner of the garage. She had spotted a baby rattler pressing itself against the concrete. I worry she'll tangle with an adult rattler."

"I'd stay away from hiking in the grass if I were you."

"I do, but Abby runs where she pleases. Last week she came home with a muzzle full of quills. A veterinarian had to sedate her to extract them."

As a city dog, Abby was unacquainted with free-ranging animals. She barked at cows and chased mule deer and pronghorn until Walter, my firstborn, took personally Abby's inattention to voice commands. Come to find out after he put her through her paces, she has known voice commands all along; she just "forgets" to heed them. We both worked on that. Now she ignores the cows that a ranching neighbor grazes on my land. As for wildlife, the pronghorn browse early in the morning and Abby watches, growling softly, through the sliding glass-door. Mule deer wander by in the evening; again, I make sure Abby is inside at the hour of their foraging. They seek out vegetation but thus far have left the baby trees alone, probably because these are closer to the house than the deers' comfort zone.

"Here, she's found hog heaven. She roams to the point of limping; she literally runs herself lame. Sometimes I give her ibuprofen in the evening so she won't hurt all night, but the next morning she is ready to run again."

"An absence of pain may be making things worse."

"My son says she'll have to figure out on her on how to pace herself."

I have seen a pair of gray foxes streak across the field and wondered whether Abby has tried to chase them; if so, she would have come up short. Foxes are way too savvy to tangle with dogs. When he yet lived in Wyoming, Walter once pointed out the foxes' den in a hollow between field and road, kits playing at its entrance. I myself would not have noticed them, but as wildlife veterinarian Walter had developed an eye. The den is still there, for I see Abby sniff around the telltale spot. The foxes, I know, will have disappeared long before she gets anywhere near. Ditto the grassland birds she tries to chase.

"Look, she's going after a rabbit!"

"One time she actually caught and killed one. Ate half of it, without my knowing. Next morning I had to clean up a mess of vomit and diarrhea."

"Keeping a dog comes at a cost."

"I'll say."

I explain how terrified she is of loud noise, especially thunder: "Even a distant rolling will send her to the only room in the house without a window, a bathroom with sky light. She presses against the tub, shaking and panting."

Lately, though, she sometimes ventures from the bathroom to seek my presence. If I happen to practice guitar, she'll wedge her muzzle into my armpit until I relinquish the instrument. I oblige and stroke her. When I first got her, she refused to be touched.

"I've seen you around Cheyenne in the car with your dog."

"Abby loves to travel. Of course, this means hours of confinement, but we've worked out a system. She runs beside the car to the mailbox, a stretch of about a mile, then jumps into the backseat. I clip her to a doggie belt."

"They make doggie belts?"

"It permits them to sit or lie down. The previous owner allowed Abby up front unencumbered. That's a no-no with me."

In the house my guests sample the snacks and drinks I put out. Someone points to my guitar. "You play this?"

"Off and on. I'm a member of Cheyenne Guitar Society."

"I've heard of them. You must be good at it."

"It started in Germany. I took a college course in classical guitar in California."

An image arises in my mind's eye: Andy, our youngest, then in his teens, popping into the room where I sat practicing a Carcassi rondo.

"That you?" he said. "I thought it was a CD." I was playing for his dad in the pre-trembling, as the poet says, of a house that falls. That was on the central coast, the San Andreas Fault a locale and a relationship.

My guests chat with one another about owls and kestrels. Then comes what I knew would pop up: "Don't you get lonely out here? With no companion other than Abby?"

" I had someone." I hesitate. "He supported my hemp project. I thought he'd move here with me."

"Yes?"

"He prefers to live in the city."

My reply is facile. Well, it'll have to do.

"I've got friends. I sing in the choir of my church, Unitarian Universalist."

* * *

Call him Garth. He is of Scottish extraction. Sometimes charming, always interesting, he is a conversationalist who is politically astute, socially conscious, and world-wise.

"I love your columns," he initiated our email conversation. "You are the voice of sanity in this town."

"Flattery will get you anywhere," I want to reply but don't.

"Ever since President Nixon's War on Drugs, hemp has been misclassified as a Schedule I substance, even though industrial hemp contains less than 0.3% THC, the delta-9-TetraHydro Cannabinol that constitutes the psychoactive substance in marijuana," my column comments. "A bloated Drug Enforcement Administration secures its prosperity at the expense of states' rights—and common sense. Worse, in its zeal to root out the 'evil weed,' the agency enlists the cooperation of state and local law enforcement by offering training with benefits. Wyoming now boasts a warrior-cop force determined to be more catholic than the pope."

My interest in hemp lies, of course, in pecuniary considerations. Unlike winter-wheat's early growing season, hemp's begins later, thus remaining unaffected by late-spring hailstorms. Its rapid growth crowds out weeds, eliminating the chemicals to kill them. Plus, it needs neither irrigation nor fertilizer.

"The DEA's Domestic Cannabis Eradication and Suppression Program (DCE/SP) is the drug war unleashed on ditchweed. Eradication chemicals are harmful to the health and safety of residents, inflict untold damage on the environment, and burden taxpayers with unreasonable costs. Ditchweed does not contribute to the black-market marijuana trade—a market that would not exist if weed were regulated like tobacco or alcohol. Ditchweed, a wild-growing hemp, is no threat to public safety. But tell that to the agency! In 1996 alone, the DEA spent over $9 million on eradication efforts in all 50 states. This figure does not include the cost of state and local participation."

To get to know me, Garth joined my "Climate Parents" group, a body of parents and educators outraged at Wyoming legislators' opposition to the teaching of climate science. Eventually he helped me lobby the lawmakers of Wyoming's Agriculture Committee. Inasmuch as we both lived in Cheyenne, attending legislative sessions was a matter of planning.

"Growing hemp was legal in the U.S. until 1957. Today, half of the 50 states have laws that allow for some form of hemp production. Why not Wyoming? George Washington grew hemp at Mount Vernon. So did Thomas Jefferson at Monticello. Benjamin Franklin used it to start one of America's first paper mills."

While I speak, Garth hands out a National Hemp Association leaflet with graphs of states that are charting their own course. It explains outdated, cumbersome federal regulations—and the inability or unwillingness of Congress to change them.

"The American Farm Bureau Federation, the National Farmers Union, and the National Association of State Departments of Agriculture all support industrial hemp agriculture. It'll create thousands of jobs. Kentucky, once the nation's top hemp-producing state, has started growing hemp again."

I refrain from mentioning that Kentucky's state police vowed to resume its fly-over "eradication" campaign, with Police Commissioner Rodney Brewer boasting that the year previous "we eradicated $44,000 worth of illegal plants and arrested 524 people."

Instead, I end on a positive note: "Congress enacted, and President Obama signed into law, the 2014 Agriculture Act, which allows states to regulate hemp production without DEA interference. A follow-up Omnibus Appropriations directive cuts off funding for DEA hemp- and marijuana pursuits. We may proceed unmolested. Wyoming's economy will benefit."

Our legislators seem unconvinced by our pitch; still, Garth and I leave the capitol in high spirits.

In time I met Garth's significant other, a woman considerably younger than he who, as chance would have it, was severing their arrangement and moving into an apartment of her own.

"It was our agreement all along," he said. "I'd help her through college and then she'd find a man her own age."

Yeah, sure.

Over eighteen months a relationship evolved from activism to engaged dialogue. He made sure I understood, his status as retired professor made him an attractive partner. A good-looking oldster, very tall with dark, dark eyes, he sports a small mustache and still owns most of his hair. On the other hand, there was an oft-repeated story about a dysfunctional son that, I began to suspect, served to screen something else.

When Garth mentioned "Rowan," his alcoholic benders and suicidal funks, he hastened to add that the man is "brilliant, absolutely brilliant. He left to study in Australia, saying he'd never return. In the U.S., he thinks, he'd shoot himself." He added an exposition of the son's academic accomplishments.

"My son, too, left to go elsewhere. Did I mention, his Wyoming career

began with large-animal wildlife? He was working toward a PhD in epide-
miology, an asset the job required. Later, as Wyoming's state veterinarian,
Walter was offered a job he couldn't refuse, teaching veterinary science at
Texas A & M."

"Good school, A & M. I did my undergraduate work there."

"Maybe their daughter will too, someday. I used to look after Amanda
when they lived in Wyoming. Her mother is a lawyer, now with A & M's
legal department."

In later conversation Garth confided a setback in another country that
entailed serious financial losses. "When I got back I sat in my house and
cried and cried," he said. It made me think maybe my impression was
wrong that he preferred surface relationships. Hence I was delighted—
more than that, surprised and elated—a few months later, when Garth
said, "I love you." The occasion, however, and the manner in which the
comment was offered, gave a moment's pause.

The occasion was this. From spending two winter months in Texas I
returned with several bags of pecans. One was for Garth, for which I anticipated a "Gee, thanks." Instead he said, "Let me count the ways I love you."

Let me count the ways I love you. What a way to convey emotion!
I imagine he figured I'd recognize the phrase as a take-off on a Barrett-Browning poem; he knew that my last (and fourth) career was
teaching college English. The utterance is a delightful riff; nevertheless,
it seemed a bit contrived. Had he used the line before? I determined to
ask what exactly he meant with his Barrett-Browning paraphrase. Sadly,
I never got the chance.

It's not often that someone we've come to value utters an "I love you."
When it does happen, it serves as a powerful motivator. But then, inex-
plicably he said he needed to visit his son.

"When things get bad, Rowan's wife emails me. I pack up to go see him."

"In Australia?"

"Or Japan. Or Belgium. Wherever he happens to be. This will be my
twenty-third time."

"I see." Actually, I did not see at all. I did, however, think of Laura Griffith's "Recover Wyoming."

"Would you agree to talk with a friend of mine? Laura Griffith spent decades abusing alcohol—and I mean abusing. At a fundraiser she confessed, what—a gallon of bourbon a week? She was past fifty before her life turned around."

"Where does she live?"

"In Cheyenne. Five years ago she founded a non-profit that helps addicts who have completed rehab. Release from rehab is a vulnerable time because people are often without resources. Laura says her own family disowned her during her down time."

"Rowan has been through rehab. Several times."

"Will you talk with her?"

"If you can set up something between now and Wednesday. I fly out Wednesday."

Laura agreed to see us on short notice. After a thumbnail sketch of her own experience, she said: "Edith tells me your son has been in rehab before."

"Repeatedly. Two weeks here, three weeks there."

"I did the same thing, but two weeks doesn't cut it. Four weeks doesn't. It took me ten weeks for rehab to take hold." Then she said, "Tell us what you do when you travel to see your son."

"He trusts me, Counselor. I hold him and hug him close. Throw out his booze. Take away his credit cards."

"You may want to rethink the booze and the credit cards. Your son must be willing—and able—to call it quits on his own."

Garth remained controlled and suave. He continued to address Laura with "Counselor," jotted down notes, promised an update on his return.

When he returned, his ex stayed over after picking him up at the airport. A week later came another frantic note from his daughter-in-law.

I emailed, suggesting he consider the term "complicated grief disorder" as applicable to his son's—perhaps his own—existence, urging he reflect upon Laura Griffith's doubts regarding his band-aid approach to Rowan's problems.

"You may be unable to grasp what troubles your son until you take a close look at whatever went on in the first year(s) of your own life. A variant may have happened to him."

From my own painful past I have learned the pervasiveness of grief. I also know something about the repetition compulsions that can emerge in family dynamics.

"My brother Helmut killed himself in Idaho at 32," I confided one time. "Repeating our youngest brother's suicide in Germany at age 18, to which Helmut was witness."

Garth seemed uninterested in Helmut and Reiner; hence, I kept quiet about Karl. Karl who had wandered with me through childhood as through a garden laid waste; Karl, closest to me in age and psychological make-up, closest also in physical locale—Karl and family settled in California, near the town where Darold and I raised our three children. Karl who managed to hang on until 45, when his demise struck me as ritualistic reenactment of Mother's death. Just as she did, Karl left behind children who find life difficult.

Years would pass, decades, before I was to free myself of the self-absorption of grieving. Similar fixations informed my parents as they lived out their lives in Germany, I now understand. Largely unacknowledged by the other spouse, each mourned bereavements that, though we children had learned of the losses, proved all but disabling. Grief not validated can be devastating, to the mourning individual as to the group she or he deems family.

"I'll never get old," Mother used to say. "I'll die of cancer like my mother did." Was her fatalistic outlook a form of grieving? Grieving for the mother lost too soon, for her own anticipated demise?

Apparently Garth is unwilling to tolerate any doubt that pertains to his actions, decisions, or relationships. I was to find, his "I love you" screened a punitiveness that put an end to our conversations.

"I'm not interested. No hugging, no kissing, you hear? I'm a one-woman man," he said after his ex had left.

He probably knew I recognized his one-woman claim for what it is. When it suits his purpose, Garth readily avails himself of poetic license; also, he likes to act the man about town. Nothing doing but relinquish a friendship I hoped would deepen with time. Whatever possessed me to imagine a life together? It was a fantasy, sweet while it lasted but fantasy nonetheless.

"We are all damaged goods," I want to tell him. "All of us. This is so sad."

Our losses, though part of life, do take their toll; we must accord them respect even as we remind ourselves: It's time to let go.

"Everything passes," comments Erich Maria Remarque at conclusion of his final novel, a thinly-disguised autobiography of a German expat who lives out his last days in California. "Everything passes and man is the only animal who knows it."

There'll come a moment when we relinquish everything we cling to: our loved ones, our possessions and acquisitions, our deeply-felt emotions. At the point of death, willingly or not, we let go of all that is dear. There is but one thing in life, and it is to let go.

* * *

My middle son, a technical writer with family in California, has helped me create a website. In it I explain hemp: It is cheap to tend, doesn't need pesticides, and is actually good for the soil. It is heartier than other mono-crops and produces the strongest natural fiber in the world. In Europe, auto makers and clothiers use it to good effect.

Problem is, until the laws change in Wyoming, hemp can't be grown here. Because the plant is in the cannabis family, for decades it has been misclassified as a drug. To this day it is banned under the federal Controlled Substances Act. Individual states have formulated their own prohibitions.

Oddly, ours is the only industrialized country that bans hemp while consuming the world's largest volume of hemp products. Industry figures show total U.S. sales of products containing hemp to be around $500 million. Australians and Canadians use hemp domestically and export it as food and biofuel. A few years ago a "Hemp Car" toured the U.S., logging thousands of miles on hemp biofuel at 27 mpg; "Hemp-4Fuel" shows the car on YouTube. At Whole Foods, consumers purchase hemp's numerous—and pricey—products: cooking oil, milk, protein powder, granola, and a variety of beauty products. Their labels indicate their origin in Canada, including the base product for the hemp milk made in Oregon.

I alert readers to "Hemp Traders," a California company that has flourished these twenty-five years. Founder Lawrence Serbin, then a newly-minted college graduate, desired to undertake something that would make the world a better place. "Hemp Traders" offers anything from raw hemp to textiles fashioned from hemp.

Its website statement, "We grow our own hemp," prompted me to telephone the company. In no time I found myself speaking to Mr. Serbin himself, who disclosed that the company's hemp grows in China.

"Most of what we sell comes from China. For twenty-three years I've traveled to that country, at least once a year, sometimes participating in hemp harvests." Indeed, his website shows him with his Chinese partner, hemp fields in background.

I asked if he envisioned purchasing U.S. hemp. He'd love to, he said, but the lack of infrastructure makes it difficult to process and ship the material domestically. On the other hand, securing it from abroad presents its own challenges.

"In China at the moment, hemp fiber is in short supply," he said, "because China has curtailed its cotton-production on account of its water- and fertilizer needs. If you had large quantities of good-quality stuff, the Chinese would buy it from you. Yes, if our farmers were able to grow hemp, I'd see about getting some of my products from them."

In February 2015, Wyoming legislators approved Leland Christensen's "Hemp Extract" bill. In this they followed Utah's lead, which followed Colorado's lead in approving CBD oil, a hemp-leaf extract more effective than pharmaceuticals in alleviating seizures, particularly in children. Utah patterned its "Charlee's Law" after Colorado's "Charlotte's Web." Both laws were named after seizure-prone little girls. However, where Colorado and Utah simultaneously enacted laws authorizing the growing of hemp, Wyoming held back. The reason? Attorney General Peter Michael, in his capacity as Commissioner of Drugs and Substance Control, advised Governor Mead not to sign the bill. Fortunately, because the governor refrained from vetoing it, the legislative effort still became law.

Mr. Michael's hobby, by the way, is gardening for organic produce.

Of Prey and Predators
Echo Klaproth

By virtue of the fact that he was born the first son of a third generation Wyoming rancher, it was an unspoken given that Jerry Moore was a "chosen one." He would be the next overseer of whatever livestock and land holdings his father had acquired in his lifetime. Whether Jerry ever gave it much thought or not, or whether he regarded this birthright a blessing or a curse, most likely depended on his age or what was happening on 9-Mile land at the time.

What was fated: he was a man-child born of the land and expected to be a faithful steward over it. From a young age his parents trained him to partner with Mother Nature, and in northeastern Wyoming ranching terms, that meant look to the north and watch your weather; that meant be prepared for the unexpected; that meant protect the grass and water because it was the key to your business; that meant figuring ways to dig out after a blizzard.

And early on, he was taught the ins and outs of predators and prey. There were particular ways that he learned and is still learning these lessons. He grew to understand that to remain a manufacturer of beef and lamb, it is imperative that ranchers control the predators that threaten the lifestyle. Little did he know that the knowledge he gained about the mind of a predator would end up both serving and befuddling him later in life.

He began learning the finer points of predator control with a .22 to thin the rabbit or prairie dog populations, either of which can clear a pasture of grass faster than any herd of livestock. Later, with more caliber power, he began perfecting his skills on the coyotes and fox, which were a definite threat. He'd often watch a coyote wait for a cow to drop her calf so it could feed its hunger. Fox proved expert at thinning out a lamb crop as fast as they were dropped. He became skilled at studying these adversaries, watching for habits and trends, staying vigilant, knowing when to take a shot and when to back off, taking careful aim before he shot, and always shooting straight.

The ranching ethic and legacy was bred into and became as important as breath to this fourth generation rancher. Living and protecting his grandfathers' dreams became his ambition, became his life. And in the beginning it was fairly simple to honor those dreams, which were all about having room to roam and enough grass and water to raise livestock without interference from the outside world. Their words became his words: "Guard your credit; it's your most valuable asset." Their ideals were his ideals: "Be fair and honest in all your dealings." Their strategies to survive were his: "When the times change, be ready to change with them; find ways to diversify." He respected, accepted, and swore to preserve the family traditions as they'd been handed down. They were his bible.

While Jerry was still figuring out how to carry on with the natural rivals of his lifestyle, there was one detail about the ranching industry that began to cause him great concern, one he couldn't quite get his head around. *Progress* became the new and worst enemy. "It's never gonna stop," became his grumble. One can imagine the reaction in the early 1970s when the first of "its kind" came thump, thump, thumpin' up over the divide, scattering a band of sheep being moved. Without warning or permission, a "pack of two-legged coyotes"—the nicest term he would ever use when referring to any intruder—came hunting for minerals under Moore lands. As seismograph crews crept and dynamited their way the breadth of the ranch west to east, they trampled a lot of the grass that was left that fall, left holes big enough to break the leg of a horse, left scars several feet wide, left this man and his family confused as their peace and quiet and the future of the northeastern grasslands in Wyoming seemingly came under fire.

The next assault came later that same decade when oil was found under and around 9-Mile. Suddenly roads popped up here and there, leading to anteater-looking creatures that dotted the landscape, ate up acres of grass, and drank up the aquifer. However, it was then that Jerry left home for a while. He decided there was too much family on the place, and women and beer were easier to come by closer to town. Twenty-year-old arrogance wasn't looking further than to the next weekend, roping, or poker game. Besides, he was still busy setting traps for four-legged prey—those he could control; those he could do something about. He could still take out his rifle and eliminate a few of them. He listened to complaints about the intrusions, but even his mother had to admit, the damages and access fees helped them get by till shipping time.

It was only after he, the eldest and prodigal son, returned to 9-Mile for good that he came face to face with the latest and what would be his greatest antagonist, a predator of a different kind. Worse than all the worst blizzards of days gone by, *eminent domain*—ingress and egress—came swooping down from the north. Since what lay under 9-Mile was in more demand than the meat the surface provided, it seemed he faced intruders from every direction. Jerry'd never before dealt with someone who would give his word only through a written contract and then turn his back and break it. He'd never before been caught up in greed's trap. He'd never before met up with a marauder he couldn't eradicate. He hired lawyers, kept the phone lines buzzing, and fought to keep the court system honest. He called in the Environmental Protection Agency (EPA), the Department of Energy Quality (DEQ), the Bureau of Land Management (BLM), and the State of Wyoming—all agencies that he supposed were in place to protect the land and water; he found they were bound by their own rules. He ended up calling them SOBs, "In bed with each other, and full of 'Sorry, we can't help you,' attitudes."

Jerry'd always been a pretty good poker player, but none of the hands he'd been dealt prior to and since the turn of the century can beat the four-of-a-kind he faces today: greed, government control, the need for energy, and progress. To this day he'll argue that he's not ready to fold 'em, but he's found out how it feels to be the prey, the one standing in the road of progress, the one dodging bullets. Like the coyotes he's pummeled his whole life, he now paces through the days, watching the horizon, finding no holes in which to hide, seeing nowhere to run. There is no more freedom, no more peace and quiet, no more home on his own range.

As the poles are being set for a 150 foot wide swath, three-phase, electric power line that will be marching the length of 9-Mile, he sits on the divide. He used to sit there keeping watch for fires. Now it's to keep an eye on who's trampling what grass is left. Sometimes you can find him sitting at the gravesite of our youngest brother, above what used to be 9-Mile Creek, now just a dry gully. He's painfully aware of the intentions of progress: even the gravesite isn't sacred. Twice big business has threatened to move it—seems it's in the road, too.

Today, he thinks about the word "diversification" and how it's changed meaning over his short lifetime. To him, it's come to mean, "Pull myself down to their level of thinkin' to play by their rules." His argument remains, "This land is all there is, the only thing worth anything, of any value. It is what used to be our nation's food source. That's the bottom line." Because he'd been taught there were supposed to be rules and a man's word was his integrity, he found himself caught unaware by the forces of change. He says, "I wish instead of so much readin', writin', and 'rithmatic, I wish they'd a'taught us some psychology in school. Maybe then I'd know how to play this game."

He's not always sure who the adversary is these days, so it's hard to study habits and trends. Yet he stays ever vigilant, takes careful aim when he can, and gets frustrated when lawyers tell him to back off. He still tries to deal fairly and honestly but finds that he's often shooting from the hip. With the uncertainty of our nation's economy and energy predicaments, one small rancher's dreams don't carry much credence.

In northeastern Wyoming ranching terms, all this has come to mean is, look to the north but keep one eye on your back; it means be prepared for the unexpected, because there seem to be no more rules except "get it while the gettin' is good"; it seems the key to his business has been cast aside as unnecessary in a world economy where everything is imported. And he worries that this surge for Wyoming's natural resources may be the last blizzard that any member of this family will ever have to dig out of on 9-Mile land ever again.

More than a Mountain Dog
Earle Layser

> There is sorrow enough in the natural way
> From men and women to fill our day;
> And when we are certain of sorrow in store,
> Why do we always arrange for more?
> Brothers and Sisters, I bid you beware
> Of giving your heart to a dog…
>
> Rudyard Kipling, *The Power of a Dog*, 1922

Some life experiences are so moving, we are compelled to record them for posterity. Through those narratives we keep alive the memories of what we loved. Not uncommonly, dogs feature in such stories.

Tongue lolling and tail-wagging, our canine companions steadfastly rump and pant their way into our lives. They become a close and loyal part of family, adopting our lifestyle, and leaving their paw-prints on our hearts. Then, invariably, all too soon, they are gone; death steals them away, leaving us broken hearted and deeply grief stricken.

Through the window of our Wyoming home, the three peaks of the west slope of the Teton Mountains loomed spectacularly. My late wife, Pattie, mused, "We are only going to the animal shelter to look. Maybe they have a Lab or a German Shepard, a big dog strong enough for sharing our active outdoor lifestyle." A mountain dog that would tolerate challenging weather, terrain, distances, and the unexpected.

Shelters can be emotionally charged places, dogs jumping, frantically barking: "Look at me….pick me, pick me." It plucks at my heartstrings. In the very last cage, destiny quietly awaited us. It bore little resemblance to a big lab, German Shepard, and certainly not a Bernese mountain dog. Pattie later described, "He calmly walked out and sat in front of us, matted dreadlocks to floor and like an English sheep dog, apparently no eyes....love can come in unusual packages, and when you least expect it."

"Do you think he will be able to keep up with us in the mountains?" Pattie worried. A little uncertain, I replied, "I think so." A more objective assessment might have judged him an unlikely mountain dog, but our instantaneous connection with the pup had set fate in motion.

When we returned to the shelter the next morning to pick him up, we discovered a shocking remnant of the self-assured dog we had agreed to adopt. Having been bombarded with shots and vaccinations, neutered, and his matted hair shaved down to stubble, he was a pathetic looking pooch.

His previous owners had incongruously dubbed him "Killer;" complaining, "Killer kept running away." We renamed him Benji, after the 1970-80s canine television star, which we thought he resembled--- before the shelter folks had given him his haircut.

Any doubt about Benji keeping up quickly vanished. Maybe six to eight months old, he was an intelligent, twenty-five pound, high-energy dynamo that would grow to thirty-pounds. He ate the cork off Pattie's fly rod handle, and chewed her bicycle helmet. Both were repairable, but Pattie was not particularly amused. Benji, though, was sensitive to even a disapproving tone of voice. We all tend to anthropomorphize our dog's behaviors, but he really did appear embarrassed about his puppyish misbehavior.

Within a few weeks, we could let him out and re-open the door only a short while later to find him waiting to come back inside. Not a barker, he possessed the alert but calm disposition of a wise old soul; and unleashed, he stayed close. On his first backcountry outing with us, it was a beautiful cerulean-blue sky day---a day when one's spirit sings. Wildflowers were colorfully celebrating the season. Benji jubilantly burst into running circles around us in the flowering meadow. The pure joy his antics communicated made us smile and laugh.

It was not an isolated incident. Over the years, when we came upon particularly beautiful natural settings in the Wyoming wilds – ethereal alpine meadows, shinning snow patches on summits, blossoming streamside meadows—Benji would erupt into running circles around us, a happy expression on his tongue-lolling face. Clapping her hands, Pattie would cheer him on: "Run, run…" She called it "running joy circles." It was an infectious celebration of life and natural beauty.

Almost too "cute" to be an athletic mountain dog, people would grin meeting him high in the mountains on hiking and ski trails. "What breed is he?" they'd ask. We didn't know. Tongue-in-cheek, I'd tell them, "He's a Tibetan sheep dog." "Oh?" they'd say. We finally concluded he was a poodle mix, an F1 doddle or a poo of some kind, maybe. I told Pattie, "I must be pretty confident of my masculinity to be hiking in the Tetons with a poodle."

Unable to resist swimming, rolling in dirt, wading through mud puddles, or poking into burr and stick-tight thickets, Benji generally bore little resemblance to any coiffured designer dogs. Living in the moment, the prospect of a humiliating hosing down or a bath in the tub when we got home never deterred him.

If we left him with a dog sitter or friends for a few days, we were told he sat at the door or a window, forlornly looking out, waiting for us to return. When we'd pick him up, he'd sit in Pattie's lap, coolly avoiding looking at us, as if offended that we could have abandoned him like that. Talk about a guilt trip.

Benji became a mountain dog to accommodate our lifestyle, but he could have easily been a performing circus dog, too. Pattie said, "He knows a dozen tricks, his repertoire is limited only by our teaching and imagination." He was an eager, quick study: jumping through hoops, hopping upright, rolling over, playing dead, finding Pattie and retrieving hidden objects by name, running figure-eight's between our legs, downward dog yoga stretch, and much more. Along on a field project with me in the Laramie Range, Benji once provided impromptu bunkhouse entertainment for an amazed work crew.

He invented his own game, we called it "grab." Dropping his toy duck at an unsuspecting visiting person's feet, he'd patiently wait until they noticed and began reaching for it, then he would quickly snatch it away; but then he'd put it right back, encouraging them to reach for it again, only to triumphantly grab it away once more. Appearing pleased with himself, he seemed to communicate: "You humans are so slow and gullible."

For years, on road trips and in the mountains, Benji was a close and uncomplaining companion. He contentedly slept in the back of the truck, in tents, on the ground, cabin floors, friend's houses, and hotels, wherever we were. On the water, he calmly rode sitting in the canoe. Buoyed by dense fur, he was a tireless swimmer in rivers and mountain lakes. He got along with llamas and horses on pack trips, curiously touching noses with them or sharing an alfalfa pellet. He picked huckleberries alongside of us. Blissfully eating his way through the patch where we were picking, he never learned to put any in the bucket. However, in the high country, I sometimes had to put him on leash. He could not resist the siren whistling of marmots. They would laughingly tease him into breath-taking all-out chases across boulder fields and talus slopes.

He was a hoot to take on a game drive in Yellowstone National Park. Pattie noted, "Snoozing when we were traveling on pavement, as soon as we would slow and hit dirt or rough road, he'd watchfully wake up." Looking out the vehicle window at deer, elk, moose, and bison, you could feel his barely contained excitement. If they got annoyingly close, he'd quietly growl or woof his displeasure. On the ground, sticking his nose in their tracks, he'd breathe in their essence, but he never chased after them. Bears, however, were his nemesis. We could always depend on him to protectively growl and yowl ferociously when they were around.

Once when we were camped at Hidden Corral Basin within the Jedidiah Smith Wilderness in the northern part of the Tetons, Benji kept staring guardedly across the meadow toward the forest, growling and sporadically woofing his displeasure, anxiously looking at us as if to say: "Don't you smell it?"

There didn't appear to be anything out there to us. During the night he woke us growling. In the morning, I found a decidedly impressive foot-long grizzly bear track in the trail thirty feet from our tent. It had not been there the day before. Needless to say, after that, we paid closer attention to Benji's behaviors and growls in the mountains. Like Meriwether Lewis's dog, Seaman, Benji protected our camps from bears.

At the request of the Valley's animal shelter, to encourage adoptions, Pattie wrote a piece for Teton Valley News, "…And Benji makes three." It pictured Benji and described our adoption experience. It is perhaps a stretch to say it elevated Benji to "legendary," but after that locals frequently recognized him by name. Pattie claimed that while downtown, a little girl had even exclaimed, "Look Mom, it's Benji!"

Both Pattie and I had elderly parents. As time passed, they transitioned into assisted living and nursing homes, where depressed residents sometimes sat slumped over. Benji's calm affectionate personality made him a natural therapy dog. He would go around greeting each person, giving their hand a gentle lick; not in submission, but rather in a show of friendliness. Amazingly, people would sit up enlivened, smiling and remarking: "I had a dog once…" Everyone delighted in Benji's performance of tricks.

As the years passed, in spite of our healthy lifestyle and diet, incomprehensibly, Pattie and I were simultaneously afflicted with cancer. Benji helped keep our spirits alive through the difficult times. I spent ten days in a Salt Lake City hospital. Benji lived in the hospital room with us, except when he needed to be taken down the elevator and outside. Remarkably, unleashed, he coolly walked the hospital hallways staying close at heel. At night he'd softly growl his annoyance at the continual intrusions by doctors and nurses coming and going into the room.

When Pattie's cancer progressed to Stage IV, she would invite Benji onto the bed with her. He would lie tightly and comfortingly against her side, as she laid her arm around him. With his coat of long curly white-hair, she called him her fluff muffin.

Following a long and courageous battle, after Pattie was heartbreakingly gone, Benji searched for her. If he heard me cry her name, he would go room to room throughout the house looking for her, like when we had played the game, "Find Pattie." It was a difficult and sad time. More than just a pet, for me Benji was a living connection to Pattie and the uncommonly beautiful life we had shared.

Benji and I became two inseparable old dogs. He accompanied me everywhere and always greeted me happily in the mornings--- prancing around, play bowing, making mock attacks, running back and forth to the door to be let out. In my state of deep mourning, his antics helped to lighten my days. He got me outside. We did long walks on the neighborhood paths and along nostalgically familiar mountain trails. Our last major day hike together in the Teton Mountains was the 15-mile round-trip to 10,338-feet elevation Hurricane Pass.

In the autumn, approaching his 14th birthday, Benji began acting lethargic. A blood test showed his liver function to be alarmingly abnormal. No one could diagnose why. Scans followed, also with indeterminate results. When he stopped eating kibble, I prepared a special diet combining green beans, rice, elk burger, eggs, and milk. He liked it, as if to say, "Wow, why didn't I get this to eat before?" But his lethargy continued to deepen; he escaped into sleeping more and more.

Our situation mirrored Ben Moon's award-winning short film, Denali, where he had developed cancer and his dog provided healing and spiritual support. Then the dog became afflicted with cancer, and in a reciprocal relationship, the owner compassionately returned the love and support his dog had given him. Benji had faithfully been there for Pattie and me; I was determined to be there for him, too.

Benji would rally, only to relapse. We existed in a state of liminality. At the mercy of a relentless cruelty, more and more, he was being pulled apart from his surroundings. Still, he would lie on the couch close against me and lovingly give my hand a few soft licks or sleep with his head in my lap snoring gently. I was grateful for every moment with him. For the memories and all he had contributed to Pattie's and my life, I owed him an immense debt of love and gratitude.

In April, in anguished despair, I sat outside in the green spring grass holding Benji in my lap. Unable to rise, with each breath he made plaintive and heartrending whimpering sounds. Ripped from each other, he entered another world----that of nowhere, yet I still felt and saw him everywhere. Reunited with Pattie, I sentimentally picture him a young, strong dog again, wearing his happy expression, running joy circles around her in a field of wildflowers, while she urges him on clapping her hands, calling out: "run, run."

Without him, I suffer an emptiness of spirit. There are fewer reasons in the world to smile. People tell me, "Get another dog." Perhaps, in time. But how could I ever find a dog like Benji again? He was never simply a replaceable object, he was uniquely Benji, a close companion on life's myriad and challenging trails and a singular friend. Death cannot steal him away; all that we loved lives within us, kept alive by our stories.

Epigram from Rudyard Kipling's The Power of a Dog. Copyright © 1995-2013 and permission for use by Poetry Lovers' Page (poetryloverspage.com).

Death Song Just Outside of Yellowstone
Corinna German

A bleached and broken skull with rough, curled horns lies fixed under the expansive, ever-changing mountain sky. At first, the clouds are fat and white. Soon, they change into bruise-colored fiends, flashing with warning; hell-fired grief. The skull is poised to absorb the wrath, but feels only a single, cool drop—quickly vanishing into the dry, white bone. It was a bluff. A fleeting moment of worry. Rolling overhead, clouds turn into swirled cotton candy.

Here, human voices are memories—but last breaths are present, and dart about, like calliope hummingbirds. A trio of petrified wood pieces underneath twisted cedar remembers the voices. They were the Sheepeaters—the Mountain Shoshone who spoke of sheep hunting and bow-making in these mountain peaks, east of what is now Yellowstone National Park. In time, the voices became afraid, speaking of invaders and worry for the future. Pursued, hunted—their voices disappeared.

Though they are gone, other elements remain. Loose shale rocks, intensely gray and contrasting against the red dirt, hold treasures etched from centuries before. Plant fossils and pinecone imprints are signatures in nature's guestbook. Elk tracks sink deep in the clay and wind across a narrow path through the shale field—a boulder next to the trail attests to their surefootedness. A loud crack in the distance is the roar of a lodgepole pine that could no longer hold strong. It stood defiant in death, but now overtaken by a small gust of wind, it returns to the earth where its seed first began. The fall is vindictive and desperate—vowing to crush anything below without mercy.

So I lie here with head against the uneven rocks, eyes focused on the wind-ragged Rocky Mountain juniper tree with the red tailed hawk perched on the highest tip. What would it be to lie here forever? To forget about my life before, and the daily weariness and sorrow. To hear only the hawk's wing beats as it departs, and the wind's intrusion on the landscape.

Just to lie here and absorb the warm sun, feeling drowsy, my breath regular, my heart beat slower. Filling my lungs with the breaths of the Sheepeaters—and, perhaps the smoky breath of an outlaw or two galloping by on panting horses. As I drift away, the last thing I hear is a Clark's Nutcracker screaming a victory song.

Magically, slowly, I fragment into small, gray pieces. Some take off in a wind gust to the west to finally rest among the wild raspberries. More settle under the elderberry bush near a black bear muzzle, purple with juice. Some rock to the left and right as they float downward, finally falling next to a white elk antler—shed last year down in the cool, dark draw. More land right in the old imprint of my boot, barely visible now, at the place we hunted the giant mule deer lying in the cliffs. They bailed off the rocks like seasoned cliff-divers, and now, my light, gray body floats down in remembrance of the pursuit. Still more gather in a sheep trap—used by the Mountain Shoshone to corral big horn sheep hundreds of years ago.

I give in to this. This high mountain paradise of earthy sage and volcanic rock. To live among the lupine, the columbine, and the calypso orchid. Safely resting with the spirits who know me well. Here, where I've collected memories—this is now all mine to keep.

Slow rivers with small gifts
Maureen T. Dempsey

It is late June and the sun is hot on my bare arms as we unload the canoe off of the top of the car and carry it down to the Big Sandy River put-in, little more than a rocky dirt road and a muddy bank. Our sixteen-foot Kevlar Souris canoe is lightweight, only weighing thirty-eight pounds. It is a new canoe for us, made for swift running rivers, but this is only the second time we have put this canoe on the water. This part of the Big Sandy River is forty miles from Pinedale, almost closer to Farson.

We walk through the sagebrush, carrying the rest of our gear-paddles, lifejackets, food, water, and a dry bag with extra clothing and rain jackets. Stashing it in the yellow canoe, it is hidden by the brush so we head out to complete the shuttle, ten miles downstream. We think we will paddle ten or twelve miles on this outing, but the river meanders, winding along as it follows its path to the Big Sandy Reservoir. We figure on a three hour float, but rivers have their own way of determining time.

Returning to the put-in, we check out the river to discover it appears to be quiet with few rapids, the current is not too swift and the water is a deep brown color. We don't know much about this stretch of river, haven't been able to find anyone who has run it. Willows hug its muddy banks and small birds flit in and out of the shrubs and Russian olive trees growing here and there.

Launching the canoe off the bank, we sink ankle deep into the chocolate sand, getting stuck enough to remove our sandals to get going. The water is cool and not too deep, so my husband jumps out and pushes us out into the water before climbing back in to guide us into the current. Although the Big Sandy follows Highway 191, the river is below it and there is little noise from traffic. It is calm as we glide past blooming pink wild rose plants and yellow prickly pear cacti. This is a desert river so it surprises us when all of a sudden a large mostly white owl with brown splotches explodes from a willow tree and flies right over our canoe. It follows us downstream and is joined by another similar owl as the pair swoop and sail back and forth across the river. It is an impressive sight watching the two at such a close range.

Joined by three smaller black birds, the trio snips at the owls' wings and the pair fly off. We continue downstream, winding in and out, coming into a canyon where the banks get steeper and sandstone slabs are sheathing off. Swallows come out of their mud nests and have a conference above our heads, squawking about our intrusion before flying off. Estimating we have paddled at least three miles, we aren't sure because of the winding nature of the river. Staying in the deeper part of the river and following the current, we zigzag across the water at a constant pace.

Suddenly, two more of the large whitish owls emerge from a hole in the mud underneath an overhang. They too swoop and glide above our heads but the show is shorter this time, and they disappear as quickly as they appeared. We decide they aren't great horned owls but are unsure until later figuring out they were snowy owls, known to be active in the daytime. Not being serious birders, we at least know this has been a lucky occasion to see these owls at such a close range.

Slowly we make our way downstream, stopping for a snack. Thunder sounds in the distance and clouds begin to build as the afternoon lengthens. We paddle a little harder, rounding a bend to be greeted by a barking sheep dog letting his flock of sheep know we are coming. The flock is drinking at the river, and another white sheepdog rounds them up, doing his job, too. More thunder, more clouds, and this Big Sandy River seems to be getting longer.

Up ahead is a diversion dam and after scouting it we decide to portage up and over a grassy slope. The mosquitos come out in force, we stop to put on repellant and are then off again down river. Rounding another bend, the river becomes shallower and we shoal out, forced to push the canoe back into the current. Our reward is to be greeted by two sandhill cranes running up and down a beach on their thin legs, honking at us. They are so close to the canoe that we can see the red on their agitated faces.

A fawn emerges from the water, an antelope stares at us from the bank. Another shorebird, an American avocet dives in and out of the water putting on a show. A cow or two ambles by, and then a few more sheep. We think we are getting closer to the take-out, but it is difficult to tell. As A.A. Miline's character Winnie-the-Pooh said, "Rivers know this: there is no hurry. We shall get there someday."

Instead, a few drops of rain splatter on us, then the sun comes out and after a few more bends in the river we see our car perched on the bank. The mosquitoes buzz around our heads as we pull the canoe out of this lazy river. It is hot now and we are ready to be off the water, but certain we have received a series of small gifts for paddling this stretch of the Big Sandy River.

FICTION

Driving the Pass in Winter
Tim Sandlin

The first decent blizzard of winter, Clyde Walsowski-Smith and I drove my new Honda Accord over Teton Pass on our way to Idaho Falls for Clyde's laughter therapy. His wife, Heather Heidi, read where laughing relieves stress so she signed Clyde up for this class where a famous therapist teaches Idahoans how to giggle. According the therapist, Idahoans don't laugh properly. Instead of sounding like a mountain stream bubbling over moss-covered rocks, Idahoans laugh like a potato would, if a potato laughed. More of a guttural mumble—*Huh, huh.*

Anyway, driving Teton Pass in a blizzard on your way to a stress reduction session is one of those examples of irony. White outs came and went and we had to guess which side of the snow poles was paved. Naturally, as happens when plowing through a snowstorm, conversation turned to virgin winter drivers. Clyde's new neighbors from Odessa, Texas, put chains on their BMW SUV snow tires in mid-September and never took them off come wet roads or dry till a chain broke, wrapped around the drive shaft, and sent them sailing through a GIVE A MOOSE A BRAKE sign.

"Their house is up for sale," Clyde said.

"My wife read on the Internet that you should drive in first gear whenever snow is falling. She said it's the only way to avoid out-of-control hysteria."

"There should be a law against wives trolling the Internet," Clyde said. "Heather Heidi Googled a story that said coffee causes heart attacks. I countered with ten said it prevents them, but she claims her one trumps my ten and I'm stuck on Oolong."

I said, "The internet is like the Bible. You look around a while you can always find what you want to hear. And then you can ignore all the other stuff."

At this point a woman driving a brand new Lincoln Town Car with South Carolina plates blew past us going about 60. Backwards. I got a quick glance at her—30-something, copper-colored hair, squash blossom necklace over a sub-zero down parka—with her arm across the passenger seat and her head twisted to see the road behind. She did a competent job, considering she was flying up the hill in reverse.

Clyde and I watched the headlights come back into our lane as she receded up the highway in the blowing snow. As men will when they share an experience that makes no sense, neither one of us acknowledged what had just happened.

Clyde said, "Speaking of hearing what you want in the Bible, did you read about that cracker who insists his employees abide by a *Biblical definition of marriage?*"

"God, I hope you aren't turning political. Politics have become a cyst on a boil on the buttocks of America."

"I'm talking Biblical definitions of marriage. I checked it out—"

"On the Internet."

"And the proto-typical Biblical marriage is an old guy with four wives and a bunch of slave concubines. I can't find a straight one man-one woman marriage in the Old Testament."

"The guy who said *Biblical family* meant he doesn't want gay partners on his group insurance. He was falling back on that verse in Leviticus about a man sleeping with a man is an abomination, but a woman with a woman isn't."

Clyde was so worked up he slapped the glove compartment. "Have you read Leviticus? Shaving or cutting your hair is an abomination. Eating clams and lobsters in an abomination. A woman can't leave her house for seven days after her period. A child who curses his parents must be immediately killed."

"My daughter should use that verse for a screen saver."

"It even says you'll go to hell for playing football."

"English or American?"

"Any person who touches the skin of a pig must immediately kill a pigeon over clean water in a clay pot, or be forever damned."

"I don't think they make footballs out of pig skin anymore."

"Okay, only old football players are forever damned."

I considered the implications in light of an after school snack my mom used to push on me in grade school. "So what you are saying is the religious right quotes Leviticus when it says what they want to hear, and they ignore it when they eat clam chowder."

"Don't even get me started on Deuteronomy."

We came around that big sweeping curve before Glory Bowl and there was the Lincoln Town car axle deep in the ditch. As we pulled over to help, I couldn't help but notice the woman had the accelerator floored so the engine was winding up like a Lear jet at takeoff and the tires spinning like grandmothers in their graves.

Clyde and I got out, walked over, and made roll-down-your-window signals. When she did, Clyde said, "Take your foot off the gas, ma'am."

"I can't. I'm melting snow."

"You're making enough ice for a hockey rink. Ease up."

She eased up. "Arnold says if you spin the tires fast enough the heat will melt you out of any snow drift."

"And Arnold is?"

"My husband. He knows every trick to driving in winter. He once lived in Oklahoma."

I knelt to check out the tires. Clyde said, "Is Arnold the one told you going in reverse is the same as front-wheel drive?"

"No, duh. A rear-wheel drive car becomes a front-wheel car when you drive it backwards. Everyone knows that."

"Did Arnold have you cram paper clips into your tire tread grooves?" I asked.

"They provide traction."

Clyde knelt beside me to admire the hundreds of paper clips pushed into the tread grooves. "Why didn't I think of that?" Clyde said.

"Because it doesn't work."

Clyde stood and leaned against the Town Car roofline. "Your husband is out to kill you, ma'am. Give me the keys."

"Are you stealing my car?"

I said, "Why should we steal a stuck car when we have a perfectly good Honda?"

Clyde said, "Jesus said you should never brag about a Honda."

"I've got to hear this."

"John 12:49—*For I did not speak of my own Accord.*" He leaned down to look in at the woman. "We're opening the trunk so we can jack up the car and save you from death."

The woman handed Clyde the keys. "Arnold says most car jackings are initiated by Good Samaritans with an agenda."

"Arnold is an idiot," Clyde said as he popped the trunk.

And there he was. Arnold, in the flesh. I'd have picked him out in a crowd of thousands. Pastel dress shirt, skinny tie, boxy glasses hanging off a ribbon around his neck. That haircut you find on gays, missionaries, and Ralph Nader.

I said, "I'm on pins and needles to hear why you're in the trunk. Is your reason Biblical?"

"It's Yahoo News," Arnold said. "The safest place to store valuables is in the trunk."

"But you're not valuable," I said.

"First Samuel, 10:22," Clyde said. *"Behold he has hid himself among the baggage."*

I stared at Clyde in wonder. "You're not a Thumper. Since when did you learn all these creepy quotes?"

"Laugh therapy," Clyde said. "The famous therapist uses Bible verses for punch lines."

All I could think of to say was this: "Oh."

Previously published in Jackson Hole Magazine.

Mother George, Midwife
Patti Sherlock

From Effie McDermott, twenty-eight-year-old wife of Hiram McDermott, farmer, Idaho Territory, 1889:

I would have died without her help.

I believe that. The labor went fine and I wasn't in bad pain until the baby's head started to come out. Then things went haywire and I wanted to give up and die from the misery. But that woman stayed close beside me, sponging my face and speaking words of encouragement even when I was screaming like a crazy woman.

It took two hours for the baby's head to get free, and she didn't leave my side. She'd wipe my brow and whisper, "Effie, have courage. Everybody's real proud of you." That wasn't exactly true, because Hiram had left the house after the first couple of screams and didn't come back until after midnight. Even Mama had to leave a time or two and walk down by the river to get herself calmed down. But Mother George knew how to say the right thing, and it inspired me to believe that everyone thought I was brave.

When she wasn't holding my hand, she was trying to turn Robert. Even though her hands are large, she's gentle as a deer, and she kept working to ease that baby out. I figure Robert and I neither one would have made it without her patience.

There's hardly a person around here who cares that she's Negro. Or part Negro. No one knows for sure about her background because she doesn't talk about it. I've probably pried more than anyone; I talk plainer to her than I do to my sister Lucy. Lucy's got a tendency to take everything I say to Mama, and then Mama gives me a lecture about how I should appreciate Hiram and my children now that we're getting a place put together that we can be proud of. So I've stopped talking to Mama and Lucy, but I talk to Mother George.

One time I asked her, "Don't you want more than this life here offers?" I was talking about pretty things and pretty houses. I went to Denver once on the train, and oh my, the pretty big houses there and the pretty dresses on the women. Even the horses glisten.

After spring breakup, we have dances once a month until late fall. Hiram thinks we ought not to go: we're Methodist and don't dance. But most of our neighbors dance because Mormons don't think dancing is sinful. Hiram says, "They don't think plural marriage is wrong, either." But I persuaded him into going.

No one dresses very fancy for the dances. Well, the unmarried girls make pretty dresses for themselves, but once you're married and have children you don't have time to sew for yourself.

Mother George sews beautiful clothes and she looks elegant in them. She buys watered silk and lace trim and pearl buttons and makes herself the loveliest dresses. I don't know how she finds the time, working her own place like she does. I said to her, "Don't you wish you had a better place to wear those pretty dresses than the schoolhouse?"

She looked at me out of those big, warm eyes, and didn't say anything. I said, "Do you remember how it was when you were a girl, how you wanted to grow up and do exciting things and go wonderful places? And here we are in this forsaken place, working like slaves."

Her face didn't have any expression at all. I felt bad I'd been so careless. I suppose the word *slave* has a meaning to her that I can't comprehend. I forget that some people have terrible hard things in their background and Mother George is probably one of them. I've read how it was down there for the coloreds, the horrible things that happened and how mistreated they were.

If she doesn't understand what I'm longing for, though, she never lets on. She listens better than anyone. I suppose that's why she went into the kind of work she does. Because she has a big heart.

One time I asked her if she knew a way to stop the babies from coming. I know that's a sin, but I've got four healthy ones and I wouldn't mind stopping there. Go up to the Ozone Cemetery and count how many women we've lost in this valley in the past ten years, and you can understand why I want to quit now. Mama George didn't look shocked, and I could tell by her expression that she did know a way.

I kept deviling her until she told me. It's been three years now and no babies. Hiram comments on it, but I'd never tell him what I'm doing because he'd feel tricked. I couldn't give Mother George away, either. Hiram would blame her more than me, because she's a darkie.

From Sister Lucretia Sutton, plural wife of Isaiah Sutton, blacksmith:
Black crows with black crows and white crows with white crows, that's what I've always said. I don't know why she wants to be here with us and not with her own kind. One other family of nigras is here, but they're fifteen miles away, and in winter I don't think she gets together with them at all.

I'm not ashamed of my views. The darkies are the ones who ought to be ashamed. Our Prophet has told us that the dark races were cursed, and I think we can see that Heavenly Father has not favored them.

At a dance once, Madame George asked me how I liked being a plural wife. Can you imagine her saying that? I gave her a cold look, and I hope she realized how rude she'd been. The truth is, I never intended to be a second wife, and it has its difficulties. But the Church was entrusted with the principle, as well as the restored gospel, and I follow it. I don't think an unmarried woman who isn't even white needs to look down her nose at me.

But don't think it's just the color of her skin that troubles me. She's odd in other ways. My mother knew something about coloreds and their rites and ceremonies, and she said they're in league with Satan. People are starting to depend on Mother George and her herbs, but I think we ought to trust our own doctors or even Sister Lindquist, who knows something about healing plants and also is a good Christian.

My daughter Libby gets annoyed at me and says when she and Tom have a baby she will have Madame George in, like her friend Eva did. I told her, and meant it, "I don't want that woman touching my grand-child. Honor your mother, Libby," I told her, "and go stay in town at the maternity home when your time comes, and have a clean, white doctor. "

From Wendall Ritchie, farmer and teamster:
She knows how I feel about her, even if I haven't put it in so many words. I stop and visit at her place a couple times a week, and at the dances I end up talking with her most of the night.

At the last one, I asked her to dance with me. She shook her head and looked flustered. I figure she's embarrassed about her size. I've noticed though, a big woman can be lighter on her feet than a small one.

Oh, you think I should worry about what people would say? Well nobody says anything to Randall Anderson, who's got himself a Flathead wife. I think Georgia may be part Indian, too, because of the shape of her face, and she's not as dark as most Negroes I've seen. Well, no, I haven't seen many, hardly any at all. But the Bixby family, they're black as obsid-ian. Georgia's skin is the color of fresh-tanned leather and her hair don't kink much. She couldn't wrap it around her head in that big braid if it did.

I wonder if she even knows what she is. I asked her once, when we were walkin' up by the stream, what her first name was. She gave me the funniest look. I said, "I feel kinda odd callin' you Mother George or Ma-dame George, and us the same age. You must have a first name, and that's what I'd like to use." She said, "I don't know." I said, "You don't know your first name?" She said, "My family got all split up. But you could call me Georgia if you like." So that's what I do.

You thought my mother wouldn't like it? Mama doesn't mind. I've talked to her about it. Mama respects hard work, and she looks at what that woman has put together for herself and the way she's available to the women in this valley, and she figures Georgia's got to be a fine person no matter what color she is. I've only ever heard of one other woman around here provin' up on a place all by herself; most women have filed on behalf of their brothers and fathers.

Mama did say, "Wendall, I wonder if your children would feel welcome. Or if it'd be hard for them."

I asked, "Would you welcome them?" She said, "I'd love them if they came out striped." I said, "Maybe others would feel that way, too."

Look at Hiram's wife. She thinks awful high of Georgia. She puts her babies in the wagon and rides up to visit with her once a week.

You may be right that marrying her would upset some people. But I don't think anyone would try to enforce that law that says it's illegal to cohabitate with someone who ain't white. If they did enforce it, we'd have a lot of squaw men settin' around in the territorial prisons. Besides, with us getting statehood, a lot of things might change.

Yessir, if I was to guess, I'd say marriage is where it's headin'. I can't think of no one I admire more than her.

I do figger she likes me, too. I ain't had a lot of experience with women, but you remember Annie Talbot? A gentleman knows when not to say much, but she and I were pretty stuck on each other before her daddy married her off as second wife to old LaVar Pierce who's got the bank. So I know a little about how a woman looks at a man she cares for. Georgia looked at me just that way when I forced her into dancin' with me. Smellin' all pretty of lavender, she put her arm around my neck and held herself tight against me. There is for certain somethin' between us. Them brown eyes told me that.

From Bobby McDermott, nine years old, son of Effie and Hiram McDermott:
Papa teases me that I got a Negro mammy. Mother George helped me be born, and Mama says neither of us would have made it without her. Maybe that's why she likes me so good. She's nice to my sister and brothers, and to Abe Olsen and his sisters, too, but I spend the most time with her. Me and my brothers and sister go up to visit her when Mama goes, but these past few months, Mama has let me ride up there by myself. No matter what Mama George is doin', she's pleased to see me come. I've hammered boards on her barn and helped her string barbed wire and pour wax on top of jelly.

She says, "Bobby, I don't know how you got so talented." I asked her once if she didn't want to have children of her own, and she said, "But what if they weren't as helpful as you? Then I'd be disappointed."

For Christmas, she made me a flute out of willow and she's been teaching me to play it. She says I got a knack for it, and even Papa likes to hear me play.

He doesn't like me going up there so much. Says if I got time to squander I ought to spend it with my own brothers and sister. But I get my chores done fast on the days I'm going visiting, and he likes that part.

From Effie McDermott, 1890:

Madame George is dead. When I heard the news, I felt like someone had shoved a hot poker in my side.

Last night, I got on my knees to Hiram and asked for forgiveness. I told him about using that plant to keep the babies from coming. He got in a fury and slapped me, but only twice. Said he had a mind to send me back to my mother, but I pleaded and said I never would do anything like it again, ever, and as God is my witness, I won't.

He didn't blame Mother George, said I was the one who should have known better. He said he was glad I wouldn't be running off there anymore, that I'd spent too much time at her place when I had work to do at home. Everybody is having a hissy fit about the rumor, but Hiram didn't take on about that much. He's just relieved I'll be home more.

There comes a time in a woman's life when she looks at the errors she's made and yearns to start over. The Bible is full of stories of how people saw their mistakes and corrected themselves and that's what you're going to see in me. I'm going to stop wanting things I can't have, I'm going to be grateful for the good husband I've been given, and I'm going to avoid people who encourage my weaknesses.

Mama and Lucy are planting a windbreak at Lucy's place and I'm going to help them. Hiram wants me to spend more time with my mother and sister.

I don't know if I'll go to the dances anymore. One way a person can keep away the wickedness of this world is to not succumb to worldliness oneself.

From Sister Sutton:

I told Lydia, "What did I say about her being peculiar? Just thank Heavenly Father this came to light before you got in a family way." Isaiah said the undertaker told him it was heart failure, but I'm inclined to think the Lord had a hand in it. A person can't scorn God's laws without paying a price. And a person can't deceive the People of God without incurring God's wrath.

I don't think there will be a funeral. Some of us are packing up to move, because those who believe in plural marriage can't vote now that Idaho is a state. Isaiah wants to leave. Second time in his life he's moved because of persecution.

But that's not why there won't be much of a funeral. Tell me, who would go to it, in view of everything?

From Wendall Ritchie:

I don't know what to think. I don't. I'm stunned, and I think it'll take me a while to get over it.

Mama came down last night and said, "There's more peculiar things happen in this world than we can ever be prepared for." And she's right.

Mama said, "Don't let this take away from the pleasant memories."

I said, "Mama! How can you say that? They're not pleasant memories anymore." And she said, "We can't know what kind of heartache another person has. Mother George cleared a parcel of land and put up a neat little place with hardly any help at all. Never once in ten years did she turn down a woman who was birthing and needed help. That's what I'm going to remember when everyone else is sniffin' around this scandal like a pack of wolves."

But I can't feel like she does. I don't know what I'll feel when I get down the road a ways.

But I'd appreciate it if you wouldn't bring up what I told you about her and me at the dance. Don't bring it up at all.

From Bobby McDermott:

I don't see how she coulda been a man. Benjamin's daddy is the undertaken and the undertaker gets to see people without no clothes. Benjamin says all those years she was just pretending to be a woman. But I don't believe it. I used to sit on her lap and when she hugged me, she had tits. Not as big as Aunt Lucy's, but big.

Boar hogs have tits, but they never do grow out like a sow's. I don't think she coulda been a man and had tits that had grown out.

There's been so much whispering, I don't know what they're gonna do about a funeral. I like funerals because of all the food, but that's not the reason I want to go to hers. I thought I might could slip the flute into the box with her so she could be buried with it. Wherever she's gone to, I'd like her to be able to play it and think of me. I'd never play that flute again, cause it would make me too sad and lonesome.

NOTE: In Bonneville County, Idaho, during the homesteading era, a midwife called Mother George or Madame George acted as a nurse, unofficial doctor, and good neighbor, while also running a ranch of her own. Women especially appreciated the care she gave them when they were having babies.

Mother George was known for her large hands. She was such a big woman, she wore men's shoes. When she was being readied for burial, her secret came to light.

Pack
Sunnie Gaylord

In Urie, Wyoming there is a trailer park that exists among a kinked grid of dirt roads that stretch back to a barbed wire fence, enclosing a sewage pond. In winter the pond freezes and the girls call it a lake. They walk the brim stabbing at its green ice pretending that they see the faces of scared men trapped in the shoal. In the warmer months they hunt for arrowheads and bird feathers, bullet casings and firecrackers. At the end of the day they sacrifice their findings into the pond and scream prayers to keep their mother safe.

Their mother, Penny, took off late in an August afternoon, with only her purse. She left everything else including the two young girls who watched her teeter through sharp gravel and crouch into a frost blue corvette, the color of Indian jewelry. It accelerated through the trailer park making a long whine. When their father returned home they explained that their mother had reshaped into a blue wolf, snarled at them and took off. There was nothing they could do.

In the weeks that followed he would take them on long drives into the Uintas to see wild bush and baby deer. The girls ate ice cream that dripped from their fists to their skirts. He would gun his truck down steep hills to tickle their bellies. Through the pines the girls would shout that they saw their mother eating bloody rabbits, to which their father did not respond.

After Christmas passed it had become clear that Penny would not be returning. They had begun to see her face frozen in the lake, her fiery hair the texture of sea foam hushed and still. The girls started to divvy her belongings. They hid her things in their room. They placed her lipsticks under their mattress and sprayed her Tabu perfume on their pillows. They wrapped her snow globes in old clothes and let them nest in their closet like large glass eggs. They hid her lighters in their jewelry boxes and tucked her cigarettes behind their ears. Their father slept at the other end of the trailer, kept up by the sounds of his daughters' howling.

Something's Gotta Burn
Jay Robbins

A man.
A man seethes.
A man seethes and gnashes his teeth.
He drives through the biting darkness
And scowls with the myopic stare of hatred.
Behold a man.
A man at war within.

Dr. Bill Perry drives a truck not his, pulling a trailer with no working lights, hauling a spooked green-broke mare with only seventeen rides to her name. His companions—the night and the white noise of KCGY. Flip phone dead. Checkbook might support a couple more bounces, but the cash is gone. A smattering of yellow legal pads and prescription pill bottles covers the dash, fogging the windows. September can be a cruel siren. Outside, the banshee howl of a Wyoming hurricane beats against the truck. Encapsulated against this frozen gale, Dr. Perry ventures forth like a pilgrim or astronaut plunging deeper into a hostile world that actively rejects invasive species.

And the northern Laramie Plains is such a world, riddled with the bones of failed homesteads. A high altitude plateau ringed by mountains, she hoards her own weather system and doesn't allow for marketable crops, save cattle. It is a desolate, isolated place, cut off and indignantly resilient. Few can live here: Indians finding refuge from whites to the south and more dominant tribes to the north; wild white men carving out their own piece of the high plains; outlaws lying low after heists; then, finally, families to claim 160 acres worth of the American dream. The handful of ranches now stubbornly residing here were built on the struggles, successes, and failures of those early homesteaders. The families who survived each new winter were able to cannibalize the homesteads of those who were unable to hang on, cobbling together a community of hardened cattlemen: resilient, stubborn, tough, and protective of their own.

Such is the land into which Dr. William Perry escapes. His presence unknown but unwelcome all the same. With the road disappearing in a maelstrom of snow, he has already become lost twice, once jack-knifing the trailer on a hairpin turn lost in the wind. What little wits the mare had left were gone as she slammed into the center barrier on impact. Regardless, the truck still drives and the mare hasn't tumbled out the back. He continues on into the storm.

The Marshall feeds into Mule Creek Road. Bill is close to the private land he wishes to trespass and trample upon, maybe leave a few gates and doors upon along his path. For decades, the cattle industry formed two branches, sometimes distinct, sometimes fluid: those with land and those without. Bill, an established large animal vet, was in the landless camp, married into a family with forty-five sections, three hundred head, three houses, on two separate plots of land. He grew up with a father also void of land, who spent his life expertly managing the herds of other people, on land not his own. Bill grew to resent the landed rancher, partly out of legitimate reasons, mostly because he was spiteful of those who were born into it while he grew up with the skills but not the money to have his own. It made it even worse to be married to the rancher's daughter. He was there. He helped. But it would never be HIS ranch. Like the prince married to a queen, he could only hope to see his offspring rise to prominence and legal ownership. That bitterness could be suppressed but not expunged. Goddammit, he is going where he pleases. *Fuck the White Man and his papers, Wild Indians aren't stopped by barbed wire.* Bill will go where he goes, *estranged in-laws be goddamned, and the pigheaded uppity republican ranchers be goddamned double.*

The Mule Creek Road passes through many ranches, some of them embedded since the olden-days, some owned as a hobby or tax shelter by men rarely seen on their own land. But these weren't of Bill's concern and were left none the worse for wear except for maybe a lit cigarette or a broken bottle. His destination is known. The terminus of the public road. His father-in-law's hunting camp and the rough country beyond. A treasure trove of place names and a veritable preserve of a stoic and stubborn Western wilderness: Ram Lamb Rock, Badger Creek, Dead Man's Meadow.

Headlights expose a heavy iron gate, the end of the road, the end of the world, maybe. A hand-painted sign: Dead End—Do Not Trespass. Bill sits and ruminates, thinking of The Code he was raised on that he would break tonight. A sigh of acceptance to ill thoughts as he gets out and fumbles with the heavy chain holding tight the gate to a weathered gnarly post. He yanks, jerks, pulls, swears, kicks. No lock, it just won't open. Just one more failure to put on his tab. He looks in the bed of the pickup and pulls out a thirty-pound tamping bar. The bar crashes against the forty-year-old sign, turning it to splinters. He is winded, and looks for a smaller tool to undo a section of the barb wire fence. A hammer. He digs the claw between the wire and corner post. Pulling, wrenching, bending the wire back and forth, forth and back, turning beet red and singing expletives while he works. The top wire breaks off, then another, then another.

"Take that, you dirty rotten cunt," he says through grinding teeth.

He opens the trailer. The mare backs up as far as the laws of physics allow, whipping her head as though a cottonmouth were underfoot. The reins have slipped off the saddle horn, entangling her front legs. "Ohh, easy girl, eaasy," he soothes. Her bobs get shallower and stop altogether. Her eyes narrow. She steps out of the trailer, thankful to be out in the open. He leads her to the cab and ties the reins to the open door. He gathers his assorted notepads and stuffs them into the saddle bag. He swings up into the saddle, as natural to him as it would be for a Mongol, despite all the broken bones and busted joints. The truck is abandoned, a sacrifice to the gusting wind.

Bill trots towards the opening in the fence, using the moonlight to guide his way. For the mare, every shadow is a predator coiled and ready to bite into her windpipe. Bill squeezes with his heels and goads his reluctant mare through the gap. She stumbles on the bottom wire that Bill missed and frantically tries to get her footing. She crow hops and throws her head. Bill swears and pulls her head around and puts her into a spin. She spins until she forgets her former fear and submits to the rider's will.

They trot uphill to the hunting house. Serene and empty. He hops off and leads her into the yard. The black quarter horse begins to graze on the dead and dying weeds, forgetting her earlier panic. Bill heads for the porch—locked. He goes to the propane grill for the spare key—gone. Another betrayal. *How dare they move the spare?* Another slight. *How dare they not trust me?* He kicks the door. And kicks and kicks, splitting the paint. He balls up his palpation hand and crashes it through the door's slat window. Jagged glass tears into his wrist.

"Gotdammit, muther," Bill moans as blood trickles down the door. He sucks in air and stifles a screech. Men don't screech and he'd be goddamned if he gave that door the pleasure. He fingers "Fuck You" on the door with his blood, and leads his skitterish black mare out of the yard.

They walk for a while along a two-lane road, used to move haying machinery in the summer and ATVs in the fall. He has traveled this road many times. Horseback to move the steers, on a tractor to mow the meadows for winter feed. Even with all the anguish and rage, he still holds a sliver of pride and belonging for better years gone by.

Bill squeezes her belly and she responds with a canter. They head to the high meadow. Puffs of steam come out of horse and rider. Even in the gusts of snow, Bill can see Dead Man feed into Manse Creek. They are black against the moonlight. A beautiful sight, no matter how mad you are. He looks to the sky. In jest. In want. He isn't sure. The mare's ears twinge and twist, pin back, and perk up, like antennas trying to pick up a signal. She knows predators operate at night, and she suspects every shadow.

The winds die, leaving flakes of snow to flutter down to earth unmolested. The banshee's thirst abated, it seems. The mare calms enough to try and graze on the dying grass while they walk. Bill yanks her head up. She snorts. They come to another fence, another reminder. He dismounts and takes his claw hammer to another post, another barrier to his confrontation with God. The work is ironic yet fitting. He helped tend this fence. He put up this wire. It should be him to tear it down.

The mare grazes for the twenty minutes it takes Bill to get through the wire. She responds well enough to Bill grabbing the reins and pulling himself up into the saddle. With a full belly, she is less anxious, less alert. They leave serene meadow for tall sage. They move along a game trail. Brush scrapes against Bill's stirrups. The irrigation ditch looms ahead. The final obstacle. Too deep to drop into and damn near too wide to jump. Damn near means full steam ahead to Bill. He cajoles the jittery novice to jump the divide. She stamps and titters on the edge and tries to turn away. Bill swears. His mount balks and drops her ass, trying to back away from perceived danger. A test of will lasts many moments before Bill turns her away from the ditch. She trots away triumphant before suddenly being turned back and kicked into a run. Bill smacks her ass with a rein and comes at the ditch at a run. She tries to hold back at the last moment, throwing Bill's crotch into the saddle horn, before her momentum makes the jump inevitable. Not so wide after all.

They calm a bit for the exertion, and Bill's sudden blunt force gut ache. They slow to a walk. She tries to graze as they move along, and this time Bill doesn't bother correcting it. A flash of white bolts across their path. The mare whinnies and snorts while bounding sideways. Bill is caught unawares and is thrown hard to the dirt. His ribs crash against a rock. Floating ribs now float a little more than is advised. He fights for air and digs into the dirt. His lungs re-inflate and he lets out a labored gasp.

A little luck, the mare hasn't run off, preferring the devil she knows. He leads her to the creek, not bothering to get back on. They walk slow, some for the pain but mostly because Bill fears what comes next. He can hear the creek running. They come to the crossing where Dead Man pays its water tribute to Manse Creek. Bill wraps the reins into the willows haphazardly. He is focused on the sky, the cloud drifting across the face of the moon.

He sheds his sweat-stained cowboy hat and drops it on the sandbar. Looking down, he thinks of his father: a World War II vet, life-long cowboy, leading member of the Stock Growers Association, a county commissioner. Respected by all, or if not, respected by those who count. Dead at sixty from mesothelioma, his death sentence in the form of a navy ship full of asbestos forty years prior. Bill stepped into big shoes, or boots. He took on his father's burden while carrying his own. The weight broke him. He couldn't pinpoint when the final straw had dropped on that poor dromedary's back, but it had happened, to be sure.

He unties and opens the empty pouch of his saddle bag, the other being full of his papers. He takes off his heavy winter coat, his wool vest. His flamboyant shirt twenty years out of style comes off too. He stamps away the snow to leave a dry spot and takes off his boots (not his). The holely socks go, and the jeans, and finally his underwear, the same clothes worn for a week or more. The smaller garments go in the bag while the rest is piled up on the saddle. The mare is indifferent.

The snow gets heavier. The creek has a paper-thin sheet of ice as cover against the wind. Bill tosses heavy rocks to break up the ice. His breathing is labored, skin prickles and reddens with the wet and the cold. He looks again to the sky. To the Maker he hates. The One who took his Dad but spares drunkards and dipshits. He looks on in defiance to that Thing, that Real Mysterious Thing or magical children's fairy tale that never cut him any breaks. That Bearded-Man-In-The-Sky who has a hard-on for Bill for no particular reason but to enjoy his mortal failures and suffering. Like Adam, he is naked before a God he was warned as a whelp not to test. Unlike Adam, he is not ashamed of his nakedness. No, it is God who should look on him and feel shame. His scars are laid bare, exhibit A in the court of creation.

"Here I am, you Bastard!" His voice carries against the surrounding hills and bounds back in mockery. "We'll do this shit your way, you Sonofabitch," he yells as he throws his arms skyward.

He cries. Loud sobs men can only let out when miles from another human being. His eyes clamp shut and he prays for the first time in a decade. *I'll get as wet as you please. I'll make the cross and say the words I know. Just take this fuckin pain away.*

He jumps into the crossing, heart stutters and pores close. It shocks his system though it's only two feet deep. He drops to his knees and starts to shake. "For God n Jesus anda Holy Ghost," he stutters as he dunks his head under. He comes up with a splash and flails and fumbles to get underfoot.

"Cocksucker! Goddamned cold stupid sonofabitch," he gutters through clenched teeth. The mare spooks and whips her head back. The reins untangle from the willows and the mare runs off in terror, saddle bags and clothing left in her wake. Bill runs after her, hooks a branch and falls flat, dick in the dirt.

"Run you cunty nigger whore! I catch up to you and you're fucking dead you rotten cantankerous bitch!

"Dead!"

Bill was only ever really alive when he was fighting mad. The hate and shock warm him a great deal. Only when the mare disappears into the blizzard does Bill feel cold. A cold so deep he has no memory to compare it to. He finds one boot—the other getting kicked into the creek—, his jeans, heavy coat, and vest. Most important, the mare managed to shrug off the saddle bags. The papers inside are priceless, irreplaceable. He forgets about the socks and underwear. He wraps the vest around his foot and cinches it in place with his belt.

Bill is quite a sight. In a strange way, he is thankful for the anonymity of the dark, even if it takes his life. He trudges on, resolute, injured and frozen. His teeth gnash and chatter. *God has fucked me for the last time.*

Hypothermia sets in. Bill straggles on in a stupor. Directionless. He moves deeper into Dead Man's Meadow, only because it is easier going with the summer-mowed grass. He moves up a rise and hears a voice. Shadows and the wind playing tricks. A zephyr howling through the brush. He shakes his head and focuses on the rocky outcropping at the apex of the meadow.

A man.

"Hallo."

"H-hey," Bill responds. He is stupefied but knows he is fighting against time and losing. He quickens the pace, moving into the stranger's impromptu campsite. He takes stock of the man and his kit. Younger with a wiry build, a beard suited to the coming season. No tent. Small pack.

"I'm building a fire," the stranger says with a carefree smile, "Or trying to, at least,"

"Oh, g-good," Bill chatters.

The stranger's checkered wool hat with ear flaps looks mighty warm. So do his Carhartt coveralls. But the gloves, the gloves are like water to a dying man in the desert. Bill could no longer feel his hands or his vest-covered foot. But no articles of clothing are offered, and none asked for.

"N-name is B-b-bill."

"Jesse," the stranger pulls off his glove and offers his hand. Bill accepts.

"Hot hell, Bill, if that ain't a cold hand! Here, where are my manners." Bill needs help putting on the gloves. He can't feel but for his eyes to guide the fingers. Jesse continues his work.

"Y-you hunting? The-the landowner would h-have yer hide for that."

"No, it ain't time for that yet. Just scouting, you might say," Jesse's amiable reply.

"W-well he'll still h-have yer hide, not the-the type t-ta take trespass l-lightly."

"I'll meet with Walter soon enough; don't concern yourself, friend." Jesse breaks the dead branches into more manageable pieces. Clumps of wet yellowed hay are stacked close by, in need of fire. "I harvested a dead cedar. Should catch easy enough. But I have nothin' in the way of kindling. Do you have somethin' to burn?"

"N-n-no," Bill replied, "Just my papers." He clutches his satchel tight to his chest, rocking back and forth on his seat of granite.

Jesse stops, smiles. "What's in there, Bill, the Magna Carta? Ha, if I haven't heard everything," Jesse says, shaking his head. "Are those papers of yours worth dying for, *freezing to death* for?"

Bill looks at the leather flap, a pale grey in the moonlight. Inside is everything. Every slight, every wrong, every plan: A letter to the three banks that closed his accounts and didn't back his bounced checks; a letter to his wife explaining his innocent employment of multiple young female assistants on long road trips; rejected letters to the editor; another to Taylor Haynes' campaign manager offering his services to get a black man elected amongst a state of racists in exchange for becoming a state veterinarian; a letter to one of his lawyers he is threatening to sue; a list of chores for his adult children to complete for his next money-making scheme; a letter to his father-in-law including a bill for thirty years of consultation fees; a rambling hate-filled letter to his former helper, a man who attempted suicide after not being paid by Bill for services rendered; a detailed list of funds owed him by two separate secretaries who embezzled from his veterinary business; a love letter to his therapist, complimenting her perky tits; letters to the governors of Wyoming and South Dakota respectively, whistleblowing his poor treatment in their behavioral health facilities; a rough draft for an ad, in which Bill is running for county sheriff; a letter to Vladimir Putin offering to be the head veterinarian in their booming feedlot enterprise; a rambling apology to his niece, explaining he has no idea why she is mad; a love letter to a married woman in Montana; a complaint to the CEO of Sharis, demanding that the Laramie manager be fired; a master list of everyone that ever fucked him: ranchers, assistants, politicians, bankers, bureaucrats, bartenders and waitresses. All with doodles and notes along the borders of the yellow legal paper: 'I am a sex god'; 'I'm not manic'; 'No one knows what it's like to live inside a fragile mind.'

Jesse props up all the cedar into a miniature teepee. He adds sagebrush underneath. He pauses, stands, then goes still, gazes at the moon.

Whether he is pondering life's mysteries or just giving his knees a rest, Bill doesn't know. Jesse turns his head, looks Bill over, and looks once again towards the sky.

"Bill, something's gotta burn."

Bill drops his head. Everything is in that pouch. All he has been through. All he has left in the world is written on a yellow pad bought with pocket change. He grinds his teeth. Nostrils flare as he clenches his fist.

"I can't. M-my life is in here. They fuckin' che-cheated me. It's all h-here. All of it. Every sa-sonofabitch. Every n-nasty cunt! I'll b-be goddamned if I give that up." He clutches the leather tighter. "Goddammed," he whispers to himself.

"I hope not, Bill."

He looks at the stack of wood. He can't look at Jesse, but can feel Jesse looking at him, through him, even.

"Let it go. Give them to me and I'll get you warm." He outstretched a hand.

They hold silent, at an impasse. And that silence brings the biting cold back to Bill's reality.

He shakes, blood retreating from the extremities. He is pale, life going out of his eyes. "Fine, take the fuckin' thing. Won't matter anyway." He drops the saddle bag in the dirt. Indifferent.

Jesse opens the flap and whistles. A veritable treasure of kindling. He pulls out two fists-full of paper and stuffs them under the brush and branches. He leaves one paper stuck out, rolled and twisted. Rummages through his pack. "Damn this bag."

"Damn, damn," Jesse says.

"What?"

"Do you have a lighter?"

"S-seriously? Wha-what if I didn't come, come along?"

"Well, I guess we were both fortunate to cross paths. Equal partners in surviving the night. So do you?"

Bill has stopped shivering. His feet don't feel cold anymore; they don't feel like anything. He pulls off a glove, leans back, and wedges his hand into his coat pocket. He curls his fingers around his lighter, at least he senses he is doing so, and pulls it out. It drops to the ground. He kicks it for good measure.

"Perfect," says Jesse. Then he kneels, placing his back to the wind, shielding the paper. He pauses. A grin forms.

"What?!" Bill says.

"It's just a beautiful irony. All these painful reminders of the past. And the past is everything, is all that happened before *right now*. And this past that you carry with you all gets burned away by your own lighter. Warms the body…" he looks up, "Maybe even warms the soul." Jesse looks at Bill again. "But it ain't Sunday and this ain't a chapel, at least in the Puritan sense," Jesse chuckles and winks.

A flick and the twisted paper lights. Jesse runs the flame along the perimeter of the stack. The papers catch hold of flame and a mini inferno erupts. Whatever regret or sadness Bill has leaves like the ash remains of his testimonies, drifting into the darkness. The warmth invigorates. The heat. The heat is overwhelming. A wondrous gift. Bill pulls off his boot and undoes the belt that holds his vest moccasin. He holds his feet to the fire, as close as he dares, and feels the sweet pain of blood rushing back to his toes.

They sit in silence, listening to the pop and flicker of the fire. Bill's torn Achilles tendon ceases to ache. The metal plate in his forearm isn't cold anymore. His ribs, broken in horse wrecks and car crashes, no longer creak. The clouds over his eyes dissipate, like the fog with the rising of the sun. And his head. His head forgets. Forgets all that has brought about his pain. He stretches out his legs and lies back, clasping his hands together behind his head. A wholesome smile greets the flame, one not seen in many years.

"Rest easy, Bill. I'll keep watch."

"That's fine, just fine."

Bill's family have no problem finding his trail. From the tire tracks off each side of the road to the chewed up earth at the hairpin junction where he jack-knifed. The truck and trailer abandoned at the iron gate. His saddled mare pacing nervously in an abandoned garden, half-wild with fear. They go to the house, hoping he is sleeping one off. They see the bloody message and follow his tracks up to the high meadow. From up there they glass the hay meadows below, the ones fed by Manse and Dead Man Creeks. They see unnatural colors amongst the rocks in Dead Man's meadow. A man. They follow through the gap in the fence, over the dry irrigation ditch, and up to the rocky rise. Bill is there, barefoot. He is smiling, gazing skyward with placid blue eyes.

A man.
A man sleeps.
A man sleeps and bares his teeth.
He lies by the burning campfire
And stares upon an eternal sky.
Behold a man.
A man at peace within.

George Running Poles
Michael Shay

Two teen boys walk along the asphalt bikeway in Riverton, Wyoming. George Jumping Bull pushes a shopping cart he found abandoned in the winter-brown grass. He's wearing black sweatpants bunched over white running shoes and a red bandanna tied around his close-cropped hair. Jimmy Jones wears his black Oakland Raiders cap sideways, its bill pointing east. He milks a pint bottle of vodka as he walks. George reaches for it.

"Not so fast," Jimmy says. He slurs his words as he swats at George's hand.

"Let me try some, man," George says. "We're cousins."

"I'm older so I get more." A smile creases Jimmy's round face. A chip is missing from one of his upper front teeth, a souvenir from his father's fist.

"Where'd you get the bottle?"

"Papa."

George laughs. "Sure, Uncle Luke just gave it to you."

"I didn't say he gave it to me. I took it, and then I hitched a ride into town to share it with my favorite cuz."

"You're in a shitload of trouble."

"No I'm not." He pulls on the bottle.

"Give me a sip."

Jimmy stops. "First you gotta run ten poles."

George looks at the line of weather-beaten wooden power poles that flank the bikeway. Beyond them, open fields merge into the half-finished houses of a new development. "I just ran ten poles." He points behind him on the path.

Jimmy shakes the bottle at his cousin. George is almost a head taller and a lot thinner. "Don't argue with your coach."

"I already got a coach."

"Yeah, a city boy from back east," Jimmy says. "Doing his good deed for the Indians."

"Coach Simmons is an O.K. guy. He runs with the team, keeping up most of the time."

"But I'm your cousin." Jimmy takes another sip. "And I'm your elder, so you gotta listen."

"Ten months older."

"I was premature, born three months too soon. So I'm really more than a year older."

George stops and stares at his cousin. "That doesn't make sense."

"Sure it does. I was born three months too early. If I was born when I was s'posed to, I'd really be thirteen months older than you."

George knows it's pointless to argue. "Whatever you say."

They hear voices, and turn to look. Two white women in sweat suits head their way. They wear dogged expressions, as if they're the only two entrants in some fat-woman marathon. The taller of the two casts a wary eye at the boys. Jimmy quickly slips the bottle into his jacket pocket.

George moves the cart off of the path so the women can pass. He knows it looks odd, he and Jimmy out on the bikeway in the middle of a school day. But he could always say they were on their lunch break. The school allows you to leave for trips to fast-food joints. Most Indian kids stay put to eat the cafeteria's free lunches. George always did. It gave him enough strength to make it through track practice. And he never knew if he'd get dinner, what with his mom either working nights or out with her new boyfriend.

George and Jimmy stand quietly as the women pass by. The one closest to Jimmy cocks her head slightly, probably tempted to see what these Indian boys are up to, suspicious as all-get-out here in broad daylight. But the plump women walk on, picking up the pace. As they pull away, George focuses on their asses. But they wear shapeless too-big sweat suits and there's nothing to see.

George speaks first. "Those two need to walk a lot of poles if they want to drop some pounds. Hundreds of poles. Thousands, maybe."

"*Hop* a lot of poles, you mean." Jimmy guffaws, punches George on the arm. "Get it?"

"I got it." But he doesn't want to imagine it. Instead, he thinks about the thousands of poles he has passed in his runs all over the county. Miles and miles of power poles. When George was younger, he spent a lot of weekends with Jimmy and his parents out on the Rez. George ran all of the reservation roads.

Jimmy's father tried to warn him away from the practice. "Some drunk's gonna run you over," Uncle Luke would say, usually in the evenings after getting toasted in Riverton and driving his sorry self home. Aunt Regina—his mom's sister—would make a snide comment about Luke being the main drunk to watch out for. The fights would start and George would escape to run. Sometimes he dragged Jimmy along, just to get him out of the house. Jimmy would jog for a half-mile or so, and then slow to a walk. George would run ahead, marking his progress with power poles or cars or some other landmark, and then circle back to report to Jimmy: "five poles" or "twenty cars." And Jimmy would say, "Do five more, do twenty more," and George did.

Mostly, George ran by himself. In the dark, he ran facing traffic and kept far over on the shoulder, sometimes running through the dry grass. In the summer and fall, when the sun had yet to set, he ran with traffic, but still kept his distance from the road. To occupy his mind, George counted the litter in the fields. Soda cans and liquor bottles. Wind litter, too, hung up like ragged flags in the sage: newspapers and plastic trash bags and discarded school assignments from Wyoming Indian High.

Jimmy slips the bottle from his pocket, unscrews the top, and drinks. He brings the pint down and hugs it to his chest. "I'm thinkin' of dropping out, leaving town."

"You only have another year and a half of school."

"But I flunked eighth grade and got kept back. I should be graduating this year. I'm just gonna get a job in the gas fields. Know how much those guys are makin'? Bert Antelope got on before he graduated and he's making twenty bucks an hour up near Pinedale."

"You're not eighteen. How you going to get one of those jobs? And you don't have a car."

"I'm strong," Jimmy says. He makes a muscle with his bulky right arm. "Not as tall as you but plenty strong." Jimmy pauses, seems to be contemplating his options. "I hate this place," he says finally.

"Stay in school, graduate, and the Marines will take you."

"Did a lot of good for my father—and yours."

"Join up and maybe they'll send you to some nice place like Japan, or Italy."

Jimmy laughs. "Indians like me go to Iraq or Afghanistan to kill *muj*. Papa told me to steer clear of recruiters. Said they will promise you computers and then hand you a rifle. Said that's what they did to him before they shipped him off to that first Iraq war." He hesitates, and then says, "I'm not smart like you, cousin."

"I ain't that smart if I'm skipping school with you and I can't get anything to drink." George reaches again for the bottle.

Jimmy holds up his hand. "Uh uh," he says. "First you gotta run those ten poles."

"Ten poles?"

"Gotta keep my cousin in shape."

George shrugs. He pushes aside the shopping cart, and looks north down the bikeway. The two women are at least three poles down the path. A tall guy on a racing bike is pedaling their way. The cyclist wears an orange helmet. A big gray mustache is pasted on his face. He nods at the boys as he passes.

George asks: "Five poles up and five poles back?"

"By my calculations, that's ten poles up and ten poles back."

"That's twenty poles!"

"You can count." Jimmy bares his chipped-tooth grin.

"Screw you." George takes off on a slow trot, warming up his legs. *Ten poles or twenty, it doesn't matter because I can run any distance any time.* As he gains speed, he feels his heart kick into second gear and then third. He can imagine the blood's path through his body. Like cars on a racetrack, corpuscles jostling to get ahead, to bring George Jumping Bull in ahead of the competition. He passes the third pole and he hasn't broken a sweat. He detours into the grass to swerve around the walking women, and likes the sound his soles make as they again make contact with the bikeway pavement. The legs of his sweatpants rub together and make a swishing sound. Builds up a rhythm as he runs. Swish-swish, swish-swish, the beat like powwow drums. The sun's behind him, but he can feel its warmth on his back. He could remove his jacket but then he'd have to carry it. Best just to sweat a little. He can run in shorts and t-shirt almost any day of the year, except those days when bitter Arctic winds howl down from Canada. He can see past the bikeway and the stacked hay bales on distant fields and trailers parked in a row off to his right. He can hear truck traffic over on Highway 26, and the whine of a commuter plane taking off from the town's small airport.

He counts seven poles and then eight. He passes an old woman walking her miniature dog. The dog barks. The woman says, "Hush, Petunia." *Petunia?* Pole nine, and when George gets to the tenth pole he just keeps right on running. I'll show my cousin. Fifteen poles up and fifteen poles back to make it an even thirty. *Hell, I could run forty or fifty if I wanted.* But he stops at fifteen and turns, again passing the dog lady (yapyapyap) and the walking women and the old guy with the mustache on his return trip. He sees Jimmy in the distance, leaning against the red shopping cart.

About this time last year, George received a letter from his father. Letters were rare anyway, but a communication of any kind from his father was the rarest of things. Sidney Jumping Bull, a good grunt in Vietnam—or so they said—but not such a good father. George was only five when he and his mom fled Pine Ridge for Riverton. He had dim memories of his father looking fine as part of the honor guard for powwows and funerals. But after that always came the party, and his father was always in the middle of it, or leading the caravan bound for the liquor stores in Whiteclay (as his mom said: "white people go to hell, Indians go to Whiteclay").

In the letter, his father said he'd stopped drinking after attending a traditional sweat lodge ceremony with some other veterans. He apologized to George, writing that he wanted to make amends for the bad times. His mom—Sidney Jumping Bull's third (and much younger) wife—received a letter too. She was skeptical, but the two of them planned a July trip to Pine Ridge. Two days before departure, they got a phone call. Sidney Jumping Bull was killed in a car accident on his way to Whiteclay. Sidney had been sober, but the other driver was not. So the trip to Pine Ridge was for a funeral, not reconciliation.

When he got home, George donned his sweats and spent the next two weeks running the dirt roads and rugged trails of the Wind Rivers. He ate what he could find, even raided unlocked tourist cars and campground dumpsters. Slept under pine boughs and in caves. One day he ran all the way up Warbonnet Peak. He could see almost all the Rez from up there, and Riverton and the gray Owl Creek Mountains beyond. To the north-west were the pinnacles of the Absarokas. George saw mountains upon mountains marching off into the horizon. Could he run them all? If he did, would he find anything worthwhile on the far side? He watched an airplane, bound for the east, pass high overhead. Other planes, headed west and south, creased the sky. An eagle rode the thermals, turning grace-fully in the warm summer air. The eagle screeched, and George heard his own name. He thought he might be in the midst of a vision, the kind the elders talked about. But later, as he looked back, he knew that it was probably more hunger than spirit, his body dropping weight faster than he could feed it. He sat up there for the longest time, until a thunderstorm forced him off the high ground and he ran back down the mountain, with lightning chasing him the whole way.

George pulls up a few feet short of his cousin. Hands on hips, breathing moderately hard, he walks loops around Jimmy. When his breathing returns to normal, he stops in front of Jimmy and says, "Thirty poles."

Jimmy grins. His eyes are unfocused, his face a puffy mask. "From this day forward, George Jumping Bull will be known as George Running Poles."

"Yes, oh wise elder."

Jimmy guffaws and holds up the bottle. Less than an inch of clear liquid sloshes around at the bottom.

George grabs the bottle and unscrews the top. As he brings it up to his mouth, the vodka's odor invades his nose. It burns his throat going down. He pushes the bottle back at his cousin.

Jimmy snags the bottle. "What's with you?"

"Sorry," George says, rubbing his nose. "It burns."

"We've been drinking before."

"Beer, though. Not vodka."

Jimmy tips the bottle and drains it. He tosses the empty into the weeds along the bikeway. "Whoa." He wobbles, leans against the shopping cart to get his balance. "I think I need a ride." Jimmy throws his right leg over the side of the cart. He grabs the sides and pushes, but doesn't get very far as his left hand slips its grip. "Whoa." He pushes again, balances briefly with one leg in and one out, and the cart begins to fall. George grabs it and pushes it upright. "Thanks, cousin," Jimmy says. He swings in the other leg and lurches backwards in the cart.

George gets behind the cart. He looks down at Jimmy's Raiders' ballcap—its bill turned cockeyed, worn like big-city rappers. His older cousin looks like a little kid crouched in the shopping cart. They roll out of the grass and onto the path. He and Jimmy have nowhere to go for two hours until George's mom goes to work and they can hang out at his place.

"Let's go get something to eat." Jimmy waves a beat-up leather wallet.

"You have money?"

"Papa does—this is his wallet." Jimmy laughs.

"Damn, Jimmy, Uncle Luke will kick your ass."

"No he won't," he says. "He won't do that ever again."

George stops. "What are you saying, Jimmy?"

"You know what I'm saying." Jimmy's voice is stern, yet distant. "I just couldn't take another punch. Know what I mean?"

"What happened?" George asks. "An accident, right? A fight, right? You punched him and he fell and banged his head? Maybe you just knocked him out."

"Nah," says Jimmy. "I cut him. He'd dead."

"Maybe he's… "

"Ain't no maybe, cousin." Jimmy keeps his head lowered, talking into his jeans. "He was drunk, I was faster." Jimmy pauses. "It was once too often, you know?

George knows. Uncle Luke has battered his way through his family, even hit George more than once, back when he was little and couldn't run away.

But now George can fly from danger, run back to the mountains and keep running. Jimmy isn't equipped with the gift of speed. He can stand and fight—he was tough after all. But what good had it done? He was alive—a good thing—but his daddy wasn't.

"Push us down to the store for some food," Jimmy says. He waves his father's wallet again. "Watching you run made me hungry."

George turns the cart and pushes it down the bikeway toward the convenience store. He wants to run, just jump over the cart and head up to the hills. Tension builds in his legs, just as it does before a race. But he can't run away from his cousin, not now.

George pushes Jimmy down the path, taking one pole at a time, counting as he goes.

Prevailing Wind
Celeste Colgan

Wind—cold autumn wind—scoops dust off the Wyoming prairie, rips dead plants from their roots, rolls tumbleweeds into mountains of fiber and dirt against the north and west sides of Barbara's office building. Barbara stares out of the fourth floor window, clasping and unclasping her hands. The prairie goes on forever, unimpeded by roads, fences, or even power lines. Dust and dead weeds advance on her like an invading army.

She turned forty last week—forty years old, widowed, without promise, without companionship, without another caring adult in her life.

She squeezes her hands together, lets them go, and picks up a ball point pen, turning it end over end. What do the self-help books say? Think of the good things. She has a good job. Her teenage sons, although quarrelsome and restless, are never in trouble. Her mother is alive, safe, and although almost blind, in good enough health. Good job, okay kids, mother okay, yet she's on the edge of panic.

She had sat up in bed in the early morning—2:30 by the digital clock—her arms around her knees. Was it the wind beating a lilac branch against her window that jolted her awake? Death hammered her mind. She rested her forehead on her knees and felt old. Old people are left standing after the deaths of a long roster of people. Old people feel invisible, friendless, alone. They live in the past, arm-in-arm with memory. Events visit them.

An event had come to her last night. No dream fantasy, but stark memory.

She was fifteen, in her work shirt and old Levis, standing in the ranch yard dust in front of the porch, watching her brother Jess and his friend, thinking what a thrill it must be to have the freedom to drive around in a pickup, thinking that the two boys were going to town and would pick up some girls, maybe even girls who were in her class, these boys—Jess and his friend, Jim McDonald—so full of themselves and the idea that they were graduating in three weeks and nothing or no one was in their way.

She stood there in the middle of the yard and felt thrilled and important when Jim said they should go out, and the next time he came out to the place he'd pick her up, not Jess.

She watched the dust roll away from that black Chevy pickup with the gun rack in the back window, watched the truck turn the corner of the drive and top the hill. Through the open window she heard her mother playing *Moonlight Sonata* on the grand piano in the living room, those deep chords piercing the low sunlight of that late afternoon in May. It seemed like she stood in the dusty yard for a lifetime, feeling envy, hearing music, glowing with the suggestion of romance.

Later there was blackness, no images, just sounds—the knock of the state trooper after midnight, the mumbling at the doorway, her mother's scream, the news that Jess and Jim McDonald and a girl from town were dead, the report that Jim's pickup missed a curve and rolled. Music stopped.

After that nightmare memory, she quickly gets out of bed, stares at the wind-thrashing branches outside her windows, jolts herself fully awake, and flings herself into activity. She mops the kitchen floor, cleans out and rearranges the tableware drawer, hauls the garbage to the front of the driveway. At dawn she makes breakfast and lunches, gets the boys off to school, takes a shower, brushes her shoulder length, graying hair behind a head band, and puts on a dark blue polyester pants suit. Looking in the mirror she gives herself a smirk of dissatisfaction. The suit with its conventional, crisp lines diminishes her, makes her an advertisement for "dressed for success," confirming she is a worker, going to work—not the head of a family, not a daughter responsible for her aging mother—she is a worker, nothing more. At the office her nervous activity continues through the morning. She adds up billable hours for each of the firm's lawyers, but by late morning her energy wanes, and relentless wind chases thoughts around in her mind like blowing dirt.

The senior apartments' manager calls to ask her to check on her mother. Mae has not been coming to dinner and is not making friends in the building. She declines to participate in group activities. She has not re-sponded well to the piano-playing restriction. There are other signs that she is unhappy. Barbara needs to talk with her.

Barbara dusts all the surfaces in her office, adjusting items on her desk and on top of the filing cabinets to sit parallel with each other and with the sides of the furniture. She puts away the dust cloth and returns to the window, sucks in and softly chews the inside of her cheek. Staring at the wind's force, clicking the ballpoint pen in her right hand, she is alone in the cluster of law offices. Here, on the edge of town in a business park surrounded by prairie and a parking lot, most workers leave at noon to do errands or meet friends. Her own boss, the firm's managing lawyer, is busy with a client luncheon until three, he said.

She sees the new mall that has been pushed upon the prairie south of town. A new coal mine has expanded the town enough to make an enclosed shopping mall possible. Inside is a foosball arcade where high school boys idle away hours. Her boys are not among those with noth-ing better to do. Every day after school they go to some kind of athletic practice, and because they miss the school bus, she has to pick them up or arrange rides home for them.

Phil used to pick them up after practice: Phil, the devoted father; Phil, who started rigorous physical training of his boys when each entered sec-ond grade. He met them after school and took them to the park where they threw and caught baseballs. Every afternoon, Phil was there. In the fall, they shot hoops; they passed and caught footballs; and in the winter, they went to the Y, played basketball and lifted weights. Every school day, Phil was there. When the boys began playing on teams, he was there for every Friday night game. She went too. But Saturday morning Phil was gone. He returned Sunday night. Every weekend she was alone with the boys while Phil went with his buddies to arenas, stadiums, courts, and courses all over. They climbed in a light plane late Friday night or Saturday morning and attended college and professional games. Sometimes they went to Las Vegas. They holed up in a hotel and drank. Phil, the devoted father, and his friends, most of them unmarried, would spend weekends with call girls. Barbara knew this because Phil told her. He would say she should be thankful because his weekend fuck fests meant she didn't have to put out for him as much. He'd laugh.

Phil, the playboy—her choice for a husband. She used to think the small plane would crash. She wonders whether she had hoped it would. The plane didn't crash. What really happened was a surprise. One of the huge Caterpillar front-end loaders that Phil was selling backed up and crushed him. She hears the signal in her mind—beep, beep, beep.

Barbara returns to her cubicle and opens an Excel spreadsheet on her desktop. She stares at the columns and picks up a stack of reports. At first it was a relief that Phil was gone, and a relief that his parents were no longer in town—no more Phil-type influence on Paul and Nathan—but now it's clear Phil is always going to be an influence. As their only parent, she is inconsequential. Phil is the hero. She is the slave. Long ago, Phil defined her relationship with her sons.

After college, instead of marrying him and returning to her hometown, she should have sat her CPA exams and found work with a big accounting firm. She should have been strong enough to strike out on her own. She wasn't. Phil offered a way back to the place she loved. He offered security. He said he'd settle down and quit chasing women; he wanted to be a father, return to their hometown and work in the family business which he'd someday own. Phil wanted her because she was steady. She'd raise children. She'd keep house, cook meals, do laundry, know her place, and provide him respectability. As the years went on, she suspected—she knew—he'd divorce her as soon as the boys were out of the house. Instead, he's dead—a strange ending to a bad choice.

Barbara gives up on concentrating, writes a note to her boss, and leaves. She has to talk to her mother. She has to get Nathan's Boy Scout badge.

In the shopping mall corridor Mae looks at her two-inch round wristwatch. Another hour to waste before show time. She goes to the next window and looks at the display by moving her head in a cross figure—side to side, up and down. Macular degeneration they call it. Mae calls it a blind hole straight ahead and a bit of sight on the perimeters. Damn tiresome. For some years after her diagnosis, she was able to hide her affliction. Once she learned the music, she didn't have to see the scores. What do sighted people know? That she could no longer be part of the orchestra? Bosh! She never missed a note. No longer have piano students? Nonsense! It was all so tedious.

Barbara left a message on her answering machine. Barbara wanted her to go to a—what was it? A Boy Scout banquet, whatever that was. Barbara, Barbara, Barbara—Barbara, meaning well. Barbara unmoored, but meaning well. If Mae returns her call, what would she say? She'd say no thanks. She doesn't want to say it. Maybe she could say she'd come over on Sunday—though she doesn't want to. She doesn't want to be around those two boys—her grandsons—all this sports, sports, sports. What's the matter with work? Those boys should have jobs, bring in money to help their mother, bring in money to pay for their schooling. But no. Barbara, meaning well, spoils her sons and interferes with her mother.

Interferes, yes, that's the word, interferes. Two months ago, Barbara appeared at her Denver hotel unannounced. She knocked on her door and came directly in. It wasn't: "How are you?" "Nice to see you." It was: "Mother, it's Barbara, I've heard you are not doing well."

Mae was glad she identified herself; otherwise, she wouldn't have known who this woman was who marched into her room. Mae offered her a chair.

"I've come to bring you home where you can live with me and the boys. We can be a three generation family and take care of each other."

Mae moved her head in a wide circle, trying to put together the complete picture of this daughter she hadn't seen for many months. She rested her hands in her lap. "What makes you think I want to leave here?"

Barbara didn't answer; she insisted. She said Mae was going to die alone in that hotel room. Social security was not enough for her to live on in a city. She'd starve or not get medical help when she needed it. She had to come to terms with her situation. She had to come home.

"Bosh! Home? What do you know about my home? I'm not going to live with you. I don't care if that Philip is dead and out of the way. I'm not going to crowd in on you and those boys—sons of their father."

Barbara kept talking about medical care and nutrition. Barbara said there were other nice places in their town to live where she could do as she pleased but have better care and be around family. Mae didn't care about doctors and meals. She didn't want to be fussed over by Barbara.

"Why are you here? Leave me alone. I resigned from being your mother twenty years ago. Go away. Forget about me."

Undeterred, Barbara played her trump card; she said she'd make sure Mae had a piano if she'd come home with her. Mae paused. She became quiet. She hadn't played since being released by the symphony. She was withering and she knew it. Playing was her existence; music was her real life; without a piano she'd die. Without a piano, there was nothing, no one anymore to keep her in Denver. She acquiesced.

Mae goes to the next store window. Maybe she wouldn't have died. Maybe she would have found access to a piano and to piano students in Denver. Maybe she could have devised a way to be a working pianist. Never mind. This is her life now. She'd figured out how to make things work for her here.

Barbara puts her SUV in gear and drives away from her mother's apartment. The manager said Mae had taken the seniors' shuttle to the shopping mall. Barbara may be able to connect with her there. Without consciously planning to, she drives to the alley house where she and Jess lived while they went to high school, where her mother and father lived the last they were together. She parks her car and turns in her seat to look out the passenger window.

A few blown-off shingles, a warped screen door slightly ajar, a single shutter lying on the ground midway down the long front yard—everything as she'd left it. She watches a magpie trying to make progress against the wind. It gives up and settles in a bramble of overgrown cottonwood branches. She loves his house. This house says: When things don't turn out the way you plan, come here.

Things didn't turn out the way Walt Rogers, her father, planned. Dashing Walt Rogers, the remittance man, tall and dark, reckless and eager, who was going to make a real working ranch out of inherited sagebrush acres; who convinced his talented wife to give up a promising music career to come live with him on the vast land; who gathered his wife, young son and daughter into a luxury sedan and drove west to lay claim to land he'd seen only once before; who hired help and bought livestock and equipment and worked every daylight hour; whose checks from Bristol stopped arriving; whose cattle starved one harsh winter; whose son was killed in a car wreck; whose pianist wife became distant, disaffected and strange; who sold everything, moved to this little house, and died. Trees bending away from gusts nod in agreement: the wind blew her father off the land, away from his dreams, away from a purposeful life.

Barbara shakes her reverie. She presses her index finger onto the steering wheel. Get back to what she needs to do: talk to mother and get Nathan's scout badge. Barbara pulls away from the alley house and drives to the mall parking lot.

Mae sits pert on the bench in front of a mall cafeteria, looking at a sandwich board sign advertising specials. A picture shows the featured items on a plate: two pieces of chicken, a spoonful of corn, mashed potatoes, and a square of cherry cobbler—all for $3.87. The chicken looks crumbly brown, cobbler gooey red, and corn, the color of a highway stripe. *You should eat. You don't have food at the apartment.* It was his voice, Roberto's, worried about her thinness. She found it boring to shop for groceries and hated to go to restaurants alone. Soon she got out of the habit of eating.

Roberto changed that. He brought food and wine to her apartment. He made her laugh. He was robust and lively—until he suddenly wasn't.

She discovered the mole close to his backbone one afternoon when they slid naked beneath the thick quilt on her bed. The next time the mole was bigger and ragged. Melanoma. He was dead all of a sudden, an abrupt conclusion to a wonderful, happy allegro.

Now she was back to no one worrying. That's all right. Oh but, Barbara worries about her. She shouldn't. Barbara is a ranch girl, knows nothing about her mother. She should work on herself, quit obsessing about things she cannot change. Her mother is a musician, and a musician chooses a solitary life. Music is better than reality.

Mae opens her handbag, takes out a small coin purse, and counts her change, identifying each coin by rubbing it between her thumb and forefinger. She snaps the small metal latch shut and returns the coin purse into her large handbag which she settles on its side across her knees. She places her fingers lightly on its surface, her feet in their canvas shoes directly under her knees.

If she looks straight ahead, she sees nothing, only hears and thinks. A line comes to her: the dead are too much with us late and soon. Or is it the world is too much with us? The next line is clear: "Getting and spending, we lay waste our powers." It's why people worry. Too much past, too many things. All this accumulation of things and memories enervates a person. When Roberto died she packed away the last of everything.

Mae closes her eyes and begins fingering the surface of her purse, swaying her torso slightly. She hears the simple melody that begins Rachmaninoff's Third Concerto. Her elbows follow her fingers running across the top of her purse.

"Playing a pretty tune, are you there?"

A southern voice comes from Mae's right. She swivels her head around.

The voice drawls, "I said. You playing a pretty tune? I see your fingers moving on imaginary keys. Watching you there makes me remember when I was a girl at my mother's place."

Mae wags her head and sights the broad smile of a woman with a spray bottle in one hand and a cleaning rag in the other. She squirts and wipes the red ceramic tile at handprint level, keeping her eyes on her work except to glance companionably at Mae.

"When we were kids on a farm in Georgia, we couldn't afford a piano, so my mother took a piece of butcher paper and drew a keyboard on it and pinned it to the ironing board. I'd sit at that ironing board there on the back porch and touch a key on the paper, and my mother, she'd sing the note. Can you imagine that? It was something. People around those parts said she had perfect pitch, whatever that means. But I never got so I could sing the note when I touched the key, so I never learned to play the piano."

Mae turns on the bench to use her left eye to help get the full view of the cleaning woman. She smiles tightly.

"You look like you hear what you play though. Must be a gift. My mother had it. I can tell you that."

The cleaning woman moves to the next panel of tile. Mae's head follows the outline of her arms which continue squirting and wiping. She smiles. Music, even unheard, touches everyone.

Leaning into the wind, Barbara sees only her feet and car bumpers as she pushes forward between rows of parked cars. Her polyester pants, flat against her thighs whip behind her legs. She pulls the heavy mall entrance door open only enough to slip inside. It clangs shut. Its crash bar butts her forward. She finds the place where Nathan's scout master works, the camera store, on the mall directory. She walks quickly, wrinkling her nose against icky smells of cinnamon rolls and caramel popcorn. She projects how pleased Nathan will be when he learns she has picked up his latest earned badge and has sewed it on his sash before the banquet tonight. No one else in his troop has a mother who would make that effort.

A skinny blond kid stands behind the camera store counter adjusting settings on a large camera scope. She asks for the scoutmaster, and this kid says, "George left at noon, said he had to make arrangements for a banquet or something. May I help you?" He sets the camera down, but looks over her head as if there were something more interesting behind her.

"But I called this morning to say that I'd be here before three; did he leave anything for me to pick up?"

"Nope, he seemed in a hurry to get out of here." He examines the aperture dial.

Barbara turns on her heel. She doesn't thank him. She didn't want to even acknowledge this callow kid. She was out in the mall corridor in a few steps. She wonders why no one but her knows about the importance of Nathan's scout badge. Deflated, she makes her way to the central atrium and sits on a granite bench by the fountain. A few pennies and nickels sparkle on the bottom of the pool. Water clear and coins bright glisten a strange awareness. George, the scoutmaster, blows her off. The adolescent camera store employee dismisses her. She's invisible. The scout badge doesn't matter. Nathan doesn't care. When she'd hand him his sash with the badge sewed on, she'd be beaming. He'd shrug. She is a fool to her son.

But she has a responsibility to her mother. She'd better find her. Why would the senior apartment manager allow a nearly blind elderly woman wander around the mall by herself? She's probably sitting somewhere in this corridor, confused.

The ripples in the fountain pool undulate over the coins in a rhythm, a melody. She closes her eyes and let the notes wash over her. "Fur Elise" breaks into her thoughts like a stream channeling through ice, melting sharp edges, rounding and smoothing hard thoughts. She opens her eyes to the knowledge that she isn't imagining music. She hears it.

She sees the crowd outside the House of Music at the end of the corridor. Something grabs her in the gut and pulls her along to the crowd. She makes her way through the people standing outside, four deep. A poster announces that Mae Rogers will be accepting a few qualified piano students beginning in January. She threads her way through the crowd and sits on a bench close to the shiny black grand piano. There is Mae, chin high, eyes closed, a dandelion puff of hair on her head, playing as if she were the only one in the room. Her dress hangs on her like hide on a winter-killed steer, but her arms and hands are strong. She commands the instrument. Mae is prevailing.

Barbara loses all consciousness of the people around her. She feels her tightness become unstrung. She watches, listens, and tries to keep surges of emotion in check, swallows with each breath. This is the music of her formative years, honest and authentic, played with intensity—clear, resonating music that she had not heard for decades—music that she didn't know she had lost. It releases her. She becomes calm, like the calm that settles on the prairie after the wind has blown itself out.

In time, Barbara looks around at others. One man has his head in his hands, an older woman doesn't check a stream of flowing tears, a teenage girl stares in rapt attention. The young man sharing the bench whispers, "I have never heard anyone play a piano like this. This music, it grips a person in the chest. Do you know who Mae Rogers is?"

She nods her head. "Yes, I know her. She's a famous pianist."

Karma
Vickie Goodwin

It was Thursday, September 23, 1976. A week until payday. I sat at the table balancing the checkbook. $32.67. It would take about $9 to fill up the car. I should get milk for the kids, eggs, bread and some fruit for lunches. That would run about $10. Of course, a trip to the grocery store always cost more than I planned because there was always that little something extra I was sure I needed. Maybe, if I was careful, we could take the kids to a movie this weekend.

We had always lived payday to payday. There was a little money in the 'crisis' savings account. With two active kids we had to expect the unexpected, so that money was strictly for trips to the emergency room for a broken finger or the dentist for a toothache. My husband, Mark, took very good care of our car. Two years of payments left until it was ours. Heck, in another twenty-five years, we would even own our home.

The door from the garage opened. I heard Mark come in from the swing shift at the power plant. Luckily, the company provided showers at work so he could scrub off the coal dust before he came home.

"Looks like snow tonight or tomorrow," he said. "The wind is blowing like a son of gun. Would you put gas in the car in the morning?"

"Hi Hon," I said. "I need to pick up a few groceries, so that will work just fine. How was your night?"

"Everything was great until about seven when Unit 3 started acting up. I spent the last four hours running up and down the stairs checking gauges and racking out fans. I am one tired puppy."

"Have a seat," I said, leading him to the recliner. "I'll get us a night cap and you can tell me all about it."

We usually enjoyed a drink together after the 3-11 shift before we went to bed. I returned with a rum and coke for him and a glass of Chardonnay for me.

"How did Debbie do on her test? We worked those vocabulary words so much she should have dreamed about spelling them," he asked. "I know I did."

"She got 100%," I laughed. "And Kara aced her math test."

"That's great. I'll leave each of them a note to read before school. Oh, I almost forgot to tell you. You remember Jake Miller?"

"Sure."

"His son, Michael, was goofing around with some kids out at the lake last weekend. They were cliff diving off Alcova Point. Michael hit his back. Right now he is paralyzed from the waist down."

"Oh my god," I gasped in shock. "Will he walk again? Isn't he only like seventeen?"

"Yeah, it was his seventeenth birthday get together. Guess the doctors don't know. Anyway, they took up a collection. I used the blank check in my wallet and gave them $20."

"Oh. OK," I said. I re-ran the numbers in my head. "We, ah, need to be careful about money until payday. We only have $10 left in the bank account." And there goes the movie and the weekend, I thought.

"I know," he said. "But, I would want someone to help us out in a pinch."

"Don't worry, we'll figure it out." I said as I took his hand. We talked about Michael and wondered how Jake and his wife would cope. We worried about our girls and vowed to never, ever let them go to the lake, or learn to drive, or go out on a date. "Let's go to bed." I said when we finished our drinks.

The next morning as I got the kids ready for school, Debbie said, "Hey Kara, I got an 'atta girl' note from Dad."

"Me too." Kara said.

"Mom, we done good on our tests. Can we go to the movie this weekend?" Debbie asked.

"You *did well* on your tests." Debbie giggled at my comment. "But we can't afford a movie this week. I will think of something fun. Off you go now."

When I got the kids off to school, I refigured the checkbook. After I filled up the car, we would have about $3 in the bank.

Time to get innovative. I mixed up some powdered milk and combined it with the regular milk that was still in the carton. That would work for cereal and maybe even fake the kids out for drinking it straight. If not, I could add some chocolate syrup to mask the taste and give them a treat. To make up for not going to the movie, I decided to allow the girls to each invite a friend over for a Saturday sleepover.

Mark got home late on Friday night. He looked exhausted.

"Bill got stuck getting out of the parking lot. A couple of us had to push him to get him going. Then George slid off the road and I helped Mike and Tom get him out of the ditch. The roads are a mess. I better plan on leaving early tomorrow. Only one more shift this week."

Saturday, the girls and I got out blankets and sheets and made a big tent in the family room. We made popcorn and orange Kool-Aid. I played Clue and Monopoly with the girls and their friends, Lacy and Susie. We changed the rules to suit our fancies. I sent all the girls to bed about 11:30. They were still snickering about how they beat Mom at all the games when Mark got home. He quietly slipped down to the family room and growled outside the tent.

"What's that?" Debbie asked, using her fake scared voice.

Kara giggled. "I think it's a daddy wolf. We better catch it." The girls piled out of the tent and on top of Mark. Everyone laughed.

That weekend it snowed six more inches. One of those wet fall snows that remind people in Wyoming about black ice and why we keep winter emergency kits in the car.

On Sunday, I made bread for the next week's lunch sandwiches. I had forgotten how much I enjoyed the process. Kneading was a Zen-like experience. After the dough rose the 2nd time, I put the loaves in the oven. I inhaled the smell of the bread baking and was transported back to simpler times in my grandmother's kitchen. I usually got to spend a couple of weeks in the summer at my grandparents' house in Casper. When I was there, my grandmother was always ready to take time to do things with just me.

I pulled down the old *Better Homes and Gardens Cookbook*, looking for a cookie recipe that didn't require eggs because we only had enough eggs left for a couple of breakfasts. A 3x5 card fell out. I picked it up, and grinned. It was the chocolate refrigerator cookie recipe my grandmother and I had made when I was a little girl, maybe six or seven. I had to stand on a stool to reach the counter.

The kids and Mark made a snowman and got in a snowball fight. Kara came in crying because Debbie put snow down her neck, so I called the girls in and helped them into dry clothes. We made the cookies while they told me about the snowman that was now a snowwoman because that is what they wanted. A couple of old scarves were the Ms. Frosty's bikini top and bottom.

"Mom, can we make snow cream? We haven't done that in a looonn-nggg time," said Kara.

"Sure." I took some evaporated milk, sugar, and vanilla from the cupboard. The girls got a pan of clean snow. Under my supervision, they added a little milk, a lot of sugar and a touch of vanilla. Then they each got a bowl, heaped in the cold treat and poured in enough chocolate syrup to float a small boat.

Monday after school, the girls asked me if I could always bake the bread for their sandwiches because 'it tastes so much better, Mom'.

"And Mom, those cookies we made are soooo good. Can I take some to share with my friends tomorrow?" said Kara.

"They have to last until Friday. If there are extras, I'll send some for your friends."

"What about my friends?" Asked Debbie. "I want extras too."

"Maybe we will have to make more," I said, laughing.

Mark helped the girls with their homework and finished winterizing the yard and house. He would start the midnight shift Tuesday night.

"Do you have enough gas to make it two more days?" I asked Wednesday afternoon.

"Oh, I think so. There's a little over a gallon in the lawn mower gas can. I'll put that in just in case. We'll be good until Friday."

And then it was Friday and payday. I paid bills, bought groceries and filled the car with gas.

We had made it with virtually no money for a week. We had fun figuring out how to entertain ourselves and make do. Mark's generosity had been returned with something much more valuable—family time and rewarding experiences.

Friday afternoon, I went out to shovel the rest of the wet snow off the walks. Lying in the gutter, weighed down by slush, was a $20 bill. Wow, talk about Karma. Maybe some new shoes for the kids or some layaway for Christmas, I thought.

When Mark left for work that night, I gave him the $20 and told him to add it to the fund for Jake Miller's son. Because when push came to shove, they needed it so much more than we did.

Reintroduction
Julianne Couch

Dear Cody,

My name is Amber Veach. I met you on campus at my college in Iowa, a few years ago. I was getting ready to graduate with a biology degree and you were a recruiter with John Deere at the campus job fair. You made it sound like working for a big agricultural company like Deere would be a pretty good fit for me. I remember you but I'd be surprised if you remember me.

Cody Cole closed his eyes and tried to summon a face. How many soon-to-be college grads had stopped by his big green and yellow John Deere booth at job fair after job fair at colleges big and small? He'd met students interested in everything from engineering to production management, accounting to marketing, to starting their own dealership. Lots of them majored in some branch of agriculture, like he had done with his ag communication degree. He didn't remember anyone who majored in biology, specifically, but there had been a lot of students. At least she'd narrowed it down for him, to Iowa.

You mentioned if I ever made it over to Moline when you were there at the corporate office I should get in touch and you'd show me around and you'd buy me lunch. I still have your card. I'm sorry I never followed up.

Ok, two things, Cody thought. She must have made quite an impression, both in grades and in…personality. Also, she must be emailing now about a job. She probably doesn't know about the layoff, Cody thought.

Anyway, I stopped by the Deere booth to say hi, but you weren't there. The young woman I talked to said she was an intern and you'd been laid off, but she knew you gave this email address out to people when you were leaving the company. I should mention I'm a teaching assistant at Sedan City while I finish my master's in biology, so that's how I knew about the job fair.

Sedan City College. Yep, that school produced some pretty good graduates for a small college, Cody recalled. But what does she want now?

So, the intern said something about you heading out to do some land restoration work in the Nebraska Panhandle, around the North Platte River basin. My thesis research has taken me out that way a few times, and I'll be heading there again soon. I know this is random, but I wondered if we might be able to talk about your work and mine, sometime.

Cody took a look at the mountains of boxes piled in every corner of his second-floor condo, getting ever taller as moving day approached. He'd lived on the Iowa side of the Quad Cities since taking the job with Deere. He had a pretty nice view of the Mississippi River from the back balcony, and even better when the leaves were off the trees. That view was almost enough to quell his longing to wake up to the Rocky Mountains every day. But in just over a week he was going to rent the condo to a guy he knew from the gym. He'd be pretty much homeless from that time forward. His mom was still at the house where he grew up in Laramie, where she'd lived alone since his dad died. His ex-girlfriend Mimi and their son Marcus were down the road from Laramie, in Ft. Collins. He'd been able to spend some time with Marcus since the boy's birth four years ago but Mimi was no longer a romantic possibility. They gave a long-distance relationship a try but both knew that shared parenthood alone did not make them ideal mates. This new job in western Nebraska would put him closer to his son, and the work was something he believed in. The downside was the USDA funding that paid for the position would probably dry up in a year. He'd be living on site so housing was paid for, plus a small salary. He'd be in one place, and not constantly dealing with undergraduates who seemed to be younger and less equipped for reality with each year he'd spent at Deere.

Some of the people who worked at Basin BioBuilders were environmental scientists, some trail builders, some range managers, some land succession experts. As communications manager Cody would be the public voice of their efforts. It wouldn't be easy, he knew, because some people were suspicious whenever private lands were opened up to the public. They worried about everything from extra littering and noise, to agricultural acreage being removed from the tax rolls, to government telling locals how to use their property. Cody hoped that as a person raised in the West but who knew the challenges facing Midwestern farmers, he'd be seen as more than just a PR talking head. He planned to get out and learn about the area, and hoped to explore the Panhandle with a little fishing and maybe even some pheasant hunting come fall.

Cody knew some of the wildlife and plant biologists who were working with Basin BioBuilders and wondered if Amber fit in there. Time to turn to good ol' Google. He clicked open a new window on his laptop and typed in her name, selecting the Image link. He scrolled past irrelevant images of pieces of amber embedded with fern and ant fossils, then there she was. Light auburn hair, freckled face, pale skin, slender, with the look of someone who spent too much time alone with plants. She was standing in what Cody took to be a prairie, wearing a Henley shirt and jeans, a backpack harnessed to her shoulders. She looked like she'd slept in those clothes. He tried to find something familiar in her face, then went back to the message.

If now's not a good time, I understand. I'll be heading out to Nebraska in a few weeks to meet with the Basin BioBuilders folks and visit some prairie sites being restored. If you are there then, maybe we could grab that lunch.

Cody reached for the cup of coffee he'd poured before checking his email and was surprised to see he'd finished it. He would make time for lunch with her in Nebraska, if the timing worked out. He'd want to know what she was working on if it was connected to the job he'd be doing. Besides, he thought, she appealed to him in that outdoorsy Iowa sort of way he'd come to appreciate. And appreciating was just about all he'd done with women for more than a year, since his most recent short-term girl-friend decided Chicago was more her style. She could have it, he thought.

Cody hit Reply to the email message from Amber Veach, keeping the subject line: *Reintroduction.* He started to type. *Hello, Amber, thanks for the note. I remember Sedan City College very well and I'm sure if we met again I'd recognize you right away. It is great that you are working on the Basin BioBuilders project. It is going to be amazing out there once they—*

Just then, his computer screen was taken over by a logo and tone announcing an incoming Skype call. Cody clicked the Close button on his email and turned his attention to the call. There was Mimi, with Marcus perched on her lap.

"Hi Daddy," Marcus said. "Look at this new truck I got." Marcus was pointing to the yellow John Deere t-shirt he wore with a picture of a bright green tractor. Cody had sent the shirt to him a few weeks ago.

"That's a tractor, honey," said Mimi.

"What's a tractor?" asked Marcus.

"That picture on your t-shirt. It isn't a truck, it's a tractor."

Cody kept quiet as this exchange continued, which was pretty common for him, especially during these Skype calls. He propped his feet up on a pile of boxes near his desk, and watched. He hardly listened to the ongoing conversation between mother and son. He just focused on the little boy with the slightly spiky hair and big brown eyes that Cody thought made his son look like a young owl. That kid needs a dad, he thought.

* * *

A week after departing Iowa, and three days after leaving Ft. Collins, Cody left Laramie heading northeast through the sagebrush prairie of Wyoming toward Nebraska. He'd take the cutoff into Sybille Canyon to visit with some researchers there who'd been part of the black footed ferret captive breeding program that Nebraska was considering in the Panhandle. But before heading east into the Laramie range toward Sybille, Cody pulled onto a two-track that led just a little way into a fishing access where there was a small parking area. He grabbed his binoculars and hiked out into the chill May sunshine, leaning into the brisk ever-present breeze.

It had been many years since he spent time in this basin "varmint hunting." His Iowa friends thought it sounded odd, but then, they also couldn't wrap their minds around the fact of so much open public land. It was his dad who'd shown him how to sneak up on the prairie dogs by walking upwind to delay detection by the colony and then fire his .22 at whichever moved first. His dad had told him about how over the years, sylvatic plague spread by fleas, combined with poisoning and whatnot brought on by ranchers who didn't want their livestock breaking a leg in a prairie dog hole, brought down their numbers. As a result, his dad explained, the black-footed ferret lost what amounted to 90 percent of their diet, to the point they were thought to be extinct in the wild. Then darn if someone didn't discover a few ferrets in the northern part of Wyoming, in 1987. The feds decided to get into the captive breeding program, and a facility went in just up the road in Sybille Canyon. It worked so well after a few years they started releasing ferrets right back into the prairie dog town where he used to target practice as a kid.

Cody sat on some flat rocks on a little rise and focused his binoculars on a nearby gap in the sage, looking for those inquisitive heads to pop up from a mound. Just like when he was a kid, on this May morning Cody could hear the prairie dogs well before he saw them, that *chee cheee cheeee* bark that meant danger is coming. He knew researchers were trying to figure out the language of prairie dogs, what the one with its head poking up from the hole was saying to its colony in the interconnected subterranean burrow beneath the sage and sand. Were they saying *look out, it's a hawk,* or *look out, it's a coyote,* or *look out, it is a kid and his dad and they have guns.*

He was unequipped now to pop one even if he'd wanted to. Once he'd started to listen for their voices and try to figure out what they were saying, he became less interested in silencing them. These prairie dogs were somebody else's problem, not his.

An hour later when he pulled into the gravel lot at the Visitor Center he learned the biologist he hoped to meet had left early to drive into Cheyenne for shopping. Cody couldn't imagine any shopping that would be better than spending time in this scenic canyon. Alone except for the senior volunteer at the front desk he took a few minutes to tour the exhibits and peer through the glass at some young ferrets being nurtured.

He tried not to think about the moment when the teeth of a mature black footed ferret hit home on the neck of a young prairie dog, but he knew that was part of what he'd be trying to protect. When these ferrets were old enough they'd be released back into the wild to match wits against their natural prey and to prove to locals that bringing them back was not only the right thing to do, it was the sensible thing to do.

Back outside, Cody found a picnic table near a fenced area where elk that had been injured and could not survive in the wild were cared for. He poured some coffee from the Thermos that his mother had sent along with him, and considered his map. He was tempted to cross public lands on gravel roads and two-tracks across the Nebraska border. It was early in the season to see newborn antelope but he was sure with his binoculars he'd be able to spot herds of pregnant does clustered together awaiting their fawns. If it was just the truck, no problem. But he had the trailer to think of so he made the more-miles but less-time choice, taking paved highways toward Nebraska.

It wasn't long before he could see Scotts Bluff, the tallest of a cluster of ancient sandstone and limestone formations that signaled his approach to the North Platte River. He thought about all the travelers, Indian and settler alike, whose lives literally revolved around that 800-foot tower. Easterners had used it to migrate west, and natives had unfurled their culture under its shadow. Maybe now-extinct animals used it to direct their movements, if that's what the fossils around there meant. Cody wasn't sure about that. He only knew his own life would be revolving around that bluff for the next year, as he would either see it in the distance or drive right by it almost every day he spent in this area of the Panhandle.

* * *

Cody had arranged to rent a small storage unit in the town of Scotts-bluff for most of what he'd brought along, since he wasn't sure what he'd have room for in the cabin. He found the place in late afternoon, filled it with things he started to wonder why he brought, then dropped the trailer at the rental place. Finally, he was traveling light, with just a dozen action packers and a few bags in his pickup. The weather was much warmer than it had been in the high elevation of Wyoming, and much less humid than in Iowa. He wondered how long it would take to get used to dry skin and cool nights at this bridge between the two.

Basin BioBuilders had been given the use of a science camp belonging to the University of Nebraska. It had a few main buildings, nine cabins, well water, and bathroom facilities with septic tanks. The mice had been gotten under control, he'd been told, and there were cell towers for phone and internet reception. He pulled into the camp about 5 o'clock and drove slowly down the packed dirt road, past some out buildings under tall stands of cottonwood, toward a flag pole he could see hung with the American flag on the top, the Nebraska flag just below it. He figured the flag pole signaled the location of the office. Cody found a wide spot in the road and parked there. He spotted a bark-covered walkway that wound among the buildings. He followed it toward a plain beige structure that had to be the office, walked up the wooden ramp to the front porch, and knocked on the door. No answer.

Cody circled around the building thinking he might see someone, or someone would see him. After the first circuit he sat on a wooden bench in front of the building and dug his cell phone from the pocket of his fleece John Deere vest. He thought about calling Louie Clark, his new boss, but instead, took a moment just to listen to the quiet. The only sound was the breeze, which sent the flags flapping and the cords clanking against the metal post. He'd never studied the Nebraska state flag before, with its seal illustrating a pioneer working some material on an anvil, green mountains in the distance. Cody wondered what caused early Nebraska settlers to come up with *Equality Before the Law* as their motto. He was thinking about whether he could find some clever and subtle way to incorporate those words into his communications about the land project when he heard a door open behind him.

Out stepped a fair skinned auburn haired woman he recognized as Amber Veach. Although Cody was surprised as heck to see her, the feeling didn't appear to be mutual.

"You must be Cody," Amber said, walking toward him.

Cody thought fast. Should he let on he recognized her right away, letting her know he'd Googled her? She saved him the indecision.

"I'm Amber. Sorry not to come to the door. I was on the phone."

"That's fine, no worries, I'm Cody Cole," he said, extending a handshake.

"I know," she said. "I mean, I emailed you from Iowa about how we met awhile back at a John Deere jobs thing. Great to see you again."

"Oh, so you're *that* Amber. I knew you'd be here but I just didn't know you'd be *here*. I mean, I got your email but was in the middle of packing. I figured you'd be in the Panhandle but didn't expect to see you *here*." He was babbling. Where did that come from?

Amber picked up a stray plastic grocery bag that was caught near the bench where Cody sat, and stuffed it into her front jeans pocket. "I know, surprise. Right before I left Iowa they offered me a chance to work for the whole summer on my prairie project, and I jumped at it. Louie and a bunch of the crew went over to Scottsbluff," she said, looking around at the quiet cabins. "There's a town hall meeting about moving the city garbage dump you can see from the Scotts Bluff National Monument area. That's not part of my focus so he asked if I'd stick around here and get you settled in."

Amber asked where his vehicle was, and Cody asked where his cabin was. They walked together up the bark path toward the truck. She stopped in front of a log cabin with a green metal roof and front porch that Cody was surprised was so level. She unlocked it and went in to open some windows while he went to retrieve his truck. He backed in to the gravel pad that served as a driveway. Together they hauled in his bags, action packers, and a garment bag in which he'd hung a few nice pairs of slacks and sports jackets. Those were there in case he needed to look professional at meetings. Getting the sense of the place now, Cody guessed that part of his wardrobe would be overkill.

A little hot but not too dusty they stood together looking at the combined kitchen and living area. A dozen flies buzzed around and Amber shooed them toward the door with a plastic fly swatter she'd taken from a hook. Cody opened a few cabinet doors and found dishes and cups, but no staples except a stack of coffee filters and powdered creamer. "You know what," Amber said. "You're going to want to go into Scottsbluff to the Safeway and pick up some groceries. But don't do it tonight. I've got some things we can throw on the grill at my cabin, which is right through those trees," she said, pointing with her fly swatter toward a stand of Ponderosa Pine.

He politely protested, she genuinely insisted. He realized he did have one thing to contribute to the meal, and that was a six-pack of warm Fat Tire beer he'd been carrying around since Ft. Collins.

"Great," Amber said. "I've got some Millstream from Iowa!" Ice broken, they grabbed the beer from his truck, and tossed the key to the unlocked cabin in his glove box. They walked to her cabin, refrigerated his beer, opened two of hers, and toasted. "To Idiots Out Walking Around," she said. "To Iowa!" he responded to the well-known acronym.

Cody tossed off his fleece vest and washed his hands and face. Within an hour they had hot coals in the free standing charcoal grill. She had several pounds of burger in the refrigerator and although they wouldn't eat that much, she'd wanted to patty it all. "People literally come out of the woods around here at night. We'll probably have some company." They shucked some corn, tossed a salad, and opened up a round of Fat Tire, now that Cody's beers had cooled.

They grilled two of the burgers, toasted the buns, and sat at her picnic table munching and talking. She told him about how she and a now ex-boyfriend restored an old house near a hiking trail in Iowa to run a bed and breakfast. She explained how business dropped off when the state stopped maintaining the trail. She said it had been hard when she and her boyfriend faced facts about their prospects, professionally and personally. Going back for grad school had helped her feel focused, she told him. Cody told Amber more about being victim to the economy, getting laid off by Deere. It wasn't a layoff in the sense that he could be called back, like a production line job would be. Laid off means gone. He told her he was ready to stop thinking about land simply as a resource for making a living, and think of it more as something to share.

Just as he was getting ready to explain that to Amber, he could hear car doors closing from across the camp. A few minutes later, two men in Carhartt shorts and Nike flip-flops came into the clearing near Amber's cabin, along with a woman in a long flowing skirt who walked over from another direction bringing a bottle of red wine. They exchanged introductions and seemed relieved to be out of the rancorous town hall discussion about moving the dump, an argument between the money-savers and the beauty-seekers. The city landfill had been there for generations and never bothered anybody. But now people were starting to build expensive homes on a hillside outside of town, and objected to garbage intruding on their otherwise beautiful view. They wanted the landfill moved, but that would cost millions, so it was probably staying put.

Amber went in to get some more burger patties, and the woman went in to open the wine. One of the guys had brought a plastic container of carrot cake to share, half gone, but still plenty fresh. Somebody brought a few armloads of chopped firewood and started a small blaze in the fire ring. Somebody else brought a guitar and a few sang some old country songs. Cody didn't want to ruin everybody's evening by opening his mouth to sing, but he was sorry when they stopped. It had long been dark, and Cody thought he should do some polite picking up of dishes and taking trash to the Dumpster at the end of the walkway. But it had been ages since he'd sat outside around a fire ring, talking with friends, without having to listen to the drone of RV generators that filled most Iowa campgrounds.

Others were starting to admit that tomorrow was a workday, though, and Cody wanted to make a good impression at his first day on a new job.

He stood and said he should probably go and organize his belongings a bit in his own cabin.

"Let me walk you back over," Amber said. "I want to show you the night."

The two of them headed single file down the soft trail. The way was lit by small pathway lights tamped into the ground along the edge of the bark. He noticed as they walked that somebody at another cabin had a blaze in a fire ring, and that the guitar player had moved over to that group. It was cool enough now that he wouldn't have minded his vest. He hadn't noticed Amber had stopped walking in front of him until he just about bumped into the back of her.

"Listen," she said.

The breeze from earlier in the day had died down, and now he could feel the creatures who shared this basin with them. In the moonlight he could see the shining surface of the shallow, sandy North Platte River, and knew there'd be trout in there. Earlier the air had smelled of campfire smoke and burger, but now he could only smell pine needles and sage. From the across the water, he could hear the yip of coyotes. He could just make out the single-note *peent* of nighthawks, chasing the early season airborne insects. One thing he didn't hear was the frogs and night insects that would be filling the Iowa soundscape over his home on the Mississippi River. He found himself thinking how it would be to own a piece of land like this, and what it would take for him to allow outsiders access. And if he did have land like this and nobody to take it over from him when he was dead, how lonely would that feel?

In the trees just above where he and Amber stood, a barred owl hooted *Whooo Cooks for You*. Amber laughed and called back, *Not me, you do!*

Cody turned to her and without planning to said, "I want to tell you about my kid. His name is Marcus."

***

It took Cody a little time to get used to the place, and the variety of the work. Some days he rode along with Amber, learning about the terrain and her research as she selected prairie plant specimens to survey. Other days he met with ranchers, economic development leaders from nearby towns and counties, and scientists from local conservation and university groups. He and others from Basin BioBuilders attended public meetings and asked for input on the land use and restoration work. Sometimes Amber would come with him. He'd noticed her habit of fidgeting with her clothing if Cody talked too much, sounding either too much like Wyoming across the border to the west, or Iowa across the border to the east. He found that not talking allowed him to listen as people said they thought the lands would be better off protected from tourists by staying in private hands. He listened to them say what the area really need was land developed for affordable housing, the construction jobs that would bring, and the families new to the area who would move into those houses once built. He heard their interest in the possibilities of how the rich habitat they lived in could be there for others to enjoy for generations.

When Cody had told Amber about Marcus and Mimi that first night at the camp, she'd said she'd like to see pictures of the boy sometime. Over the next several weeks she asked about Marcus on occasion, and when she did, Cody would try to tell a short, non-boring version of something cute the kid had said or done. When she didn't ask about him, Cody resisted volunteering information. Sometimes he'd head to Ft. Collins to spend weekends with Marcus. He didn't tell Amber he stayed in Mimi's spare room, and she didn't ask. Sometimes he'd take a day trip just as far as Laramie to see his mother. Amber didn't ask to come along, and he didn't make the offer. Before he knew it, late May had turned to August, and he still had nine months to stay there. But Amber was already mentally preparing for Iowa, prepping for a course she'd be teaching, and typing up some field journals for an article she'd be writing with one of her professors. Soon, someone else would gather seeds from the plants she'd surveyed and use them to reseed nearby cultivated land back into prairie.

The day before Amber was to leave for Iowa, Cody and a few others helped her pack up her car and clean out her cabin. There'd been a going-away dinner for her with a good meal, some wine, and lots of hugs. On behalf of the staff, Louie gave her a bright red Basin BioBuilders ball cap, with *Amber* stitched into the back, above the clasp. Then people headed back to their cabins, hiding from mosquitos behind closed doors for a few hours in these long twilight nights of summer.

Amber told Cody she'd rather say goodnight to him now, instead of him getting up at dark o'clock just to wave as she pulled out. They walked together to the edge of the camp, sitting on a log on a hillside on the edge of a stand of Ponderosa Pine, where they'd often sat together. There was just enough daylight for them to see the Scotts Bluff monument in the distance beyond the river.

Cody tapped his left foot against her right foot. "Hey, so it isn't going to be the same without you here. I'm going to miss hanging out."

Amber tapped his foot back. "Yeah, me too. You were nice to help me haul my gear around all summer."

"No really, I learned a lot. It helped me understand what this place is about and what I should be saying about it. And how I should be thinking about it."

Amber was quiet for a bit. They could hear the zinging of a few mosquitos and they both instinctively rolled down their shirt sleeves for protection.

"So," she finally said.

"Yeah," he replied.

When she didn't respond he tried again. "So, Amber. If you are up for it, I'd really like to see you again. I mean, you know where I'll be for the next ten months. I pretty much know where you'll be, in Sedan City, right?" Amber nodded. "After this, I'm not sure what's next for me," Cody continued on. "I might go back to Iowa and live in my condo but I think I could sell it to the renter. I might spend some time back in Laramie with my mom, who could probably use some extra help these days. I'm pretty sure I could get a job there."

"Oh, I'm sure you could," Amber replied. "You'd be fine. I've always liked Wyoming, and Laramie is nice. And there's Marcus."

"Yes, there's Marcus," Cody said quickly, because he'd been giving that fact some thought but wasn't sure how to bring it up. "I guess, I mean, maybe if I knew what you might be doing, we might..." He stopped talking and finally turned his head to look right at her. In spite of a summer in the prairies of Nebraska, she'd managed not to sunburn.

Amber met his eyes for a moment and then looked away, fiddling with the bill of her red ball cap. "My next year of grad school won't be easy, but I'll get through it. I was actually thinking about a few weeks hiking in Wyoming next June, to celebrate graduation. Maybe you can get away, wherever you are."

Cody let the overview of her schedule sink in for a minute. Then he took the ball cap from her hands and used it to swish away some mosquitoes around her head. She put her hand on his arm and stopped his motion. "Why don't we see how we feel after the 'grand romance' of Camp BioBuilders has faded and figure out what makes sense," she said.

They both laughed a bit at that phrasing, their awkwardness broken. They'd been good at signaling to one another their mutual attraction but hadn't put it into words. They'd both understood that this place, part summer camp and part office space, was not ideal for starting a relationship. Nobody was spending the night at anybody else's cabin, and they weren't going to go that route, either. Cody leaned over to kiss Amber. It wasn't their first kiss but this one carried extra weight. The way she pressed into him, resting her hands on the top of his shoulders, created a new shared space between them. For the first time he really understood she'd be leaving in the morning and in spite of the camp full of people, he'd be alone.

Just then, a chorus of katydids blasted out from the tree tops, triggered by dusk. *Ka-ty-did, she did, she did, Ka-ty did, she did, she did, Ka-ty did...* And then silence. What the hell was that supposed to mean, Cody wondered. He waited for a snappy comeback from Amber, but none came. He was supposed to be the professional communicator. Yet when it mattered most he communicated no differently from the katydids or prairie dogs: in short bursts of obtuseness only those of their same kind could fully interpret. He wanted to tell Amber he wished this place was theirs, that Marcus could be theirs to tend together. He wanted to say he wished Mimi could be there too, only somehow on the other side of a veil, present for Marcus but in her own sphere. He wanted to say he wished the Mississippi River was closer, and the Rocky Mountains, too, and he could fold them up like two edges of a blanket, a chrysalis for their mutual future.

Instead, he said "Look out there, past the river." He gently shifted Amber's position against him so she'd look in the direction he meant. "The way the cloud cover is hemming in the lights from town, it almost looks like we're right on top of the Bluff. Like we're alone together in a tower of trees and light."

"In a lot of ways, this is just like home," Amber replied.

"Yep," Cody said. "It is. It surely is."

The Saddlemaker
Alyson Hagy

I don't remember the night they came for me. I don't remember the muddy growl of the truck or the way the back seat must have smelled of dog. There hadn't been a dog in my life for a long time, not since freckled Dennis shacked up with my mother. Freckled Dennis had an ugly dog named Glock that liked to carry rocks in its ugly mouth.

We were in the truck for five hours. That's how long it took to get from Rapid City, South Dakota, to Lost Cabin, Wyoming, where Penny and Big Bill lived. It's an easy drive at night. Quiet. Empty. Penny told me later that the trip home was the only sure thing she and Big Bill attempted in those crazy, early weeks. Everything else was panic and prayer.

When I woke up, I thought I'd been trapped in a bright, white box. I thought the clean sheet Penny had tucked around me was some kind of angel-sized bandage. Penny apologized. They hadn't been expecting a visitor. She had forgotten to close the window blinds against the morning.

They called it the guest room. It had thick carpet the color of my mother's dancing dress and a rocking chair covered in real velvet, the kind you can write on with the ends of your fingers. The room looked like it hadn't been breathed in by another human person.

Penny said she was my grandmother. She didn't provide the details.

Assuming I had the count right, it had been four days since I'd seen my mother, Annette. That was no kind of record. She expected me to take care of myself.

Penny fed me breakfast at a yellow-topped table that was shaped like a restaurant booth. There was a glass of berry juice. There was a hot, crusty waffle and soft butter and syrup. I asked for another waffle after I unfolded the paper napkin next to my plate just the way I'd seen Penny do. I broke the rule: Don't ever act hungry. Then my puffed-out stomach tried to escape through my mouth, and there was a mess on Penny's brick-pattern floor, and I'd broken another rule, one that had been slapped into me since forever: Don't call fucking attention to yourself.

They talked about my teeth. I heard them. And Penny said something about getting my hair cut. Big Bill, who didn't seem so big to me at the time, kept his words down in the bucket of his chest. He had come into the house from the tack store that stood at the front edge of their lot, and he still wore the gold-wire glasses that slid down his nose.

"I get my teeth fixed at school," I told them. "The government pays for everything. And my mom likes my hair long."

"Does that mom of yours like the nits that have took up residence on your head?" Big Bill asked. It was the first thing he had said directly to me. The eyes behind his glasses looked watery and old, flooded with twisted shapes I didn't recognize. I was afraid to admit I didn't know what a nit was.

"Don't worry, hon," Penny said, reaching out for me. "We'll get Trish Mascarenas to fix you up. And Dr. Jansen. And we'll get you some clothes."

"I want to go home," I said.

"I know you do," Penny said with her burned-coffee breath. She pinched me into the angle of her arm like she could hear something coming for us through the walls of the house, something huge and unmarked. "But we need to do like the people in South Dakota have advised. We got to go a step at a time."

"Don't touch nothing." This was what Big Bill said when he found me in his workshop. I didn't know he could see me. I was standing against a wall hung with some kind of animal skin and some kind of clean-smelling rope. I had lots of experience being invisible. My experience didn't seem to work so well with Big Bill.

"I ain't the school principal," he said. "But I got a lot of knives and tools in here. Acids. Dyes. I don't know yet if you're the stupid kind of kid or not."

I didn't say anything. That was my favorite rule: Don't open your big mouth unless it's necessary. It was a rule I handled better than my mother did.

"You can stay if you want," Bill said. "A.J. used to spend his share of time in here before he discovered dirt bikes and girls."

I kept the position I had, with the ropes falling in front of me like the white stream of a waterfall. I had imagination when it came to my hiding places. Bill was working at his bench, tying something into shape with his hands. He was very fast with his fingers and hands. It took me a while to get used to that speed. It scared me.

"I'm finishing a bosal for the fellow who breaks colts for the Wallops," Big Bill said. "He likes his rawhide wove a certain style. I can ship this to Big Horn and have a check in my pocket by the end of the week. Your granny likes it when I pretend to get some work done."

I wasn't really listening. I had things to figure out. I needed to know how many of the doors in the shop opened to the outside. I had already discounted the dog. It never left Big Bill's side unless ordered to do so. He called the dog Mike. I could tell from the taste of the air that cigarettes had been smoked in Big Bill's shop not so long ago. Nobody was likely to offer me a cigarette. If I wanted one, I'd have to find it and steal it.

"You don't say much, do you?" Big Bill said. "When I first saw Evo Parsons plaiting out a set of reins, I thought I'd come upon the magic dwarf in that story *Rumpelstiltskin*, working plain straw right into gold. I thought it was the prettiest little chore I'd ever seen."

I closed my eyes. The cigarette smell was bringing on a bad memory, one that involved my money-loving mother.

"You know them stories, don't you?" Big Bill asked, never looking my way. "Fairy stories? The ones with giants and trolls always trying to make a mean deal and getting suckered in the end?"

I was very good at keeping inside what needed to be kept inside. My knees were shaking under the Wrangler jeans Penny had bought for me at the second-hand store, but Big Bill couldn't see my knees. Annette and me in a basement in Belle Fourche, delivering a child's pink backpack, my mother asking for a cash bonus. Jittering knees. The chain link feeling around my lungs that told me not to run. Penny had paid her friend Trish Mascarenas to cut my hair off the day before, so my neck felt new and skinny and prickling as I stood there against Big Bill's wall. I wished I had some of the animal skin hanging from that wall to wrap around my disgusting weak neck.

"I suppose you'd be offended if I asked what the hell my daughter thinks she's been doing with you," Big Bill said. "It don't look like she's accomplished much in the way of raising you up. She seems happy to prance right off the edge of the world in any way that occurs to her."

The basement in Belle Fourche was wet. It had toads in it. The man with the cross tattooed on his shaved head made sure I saw him boot-squish a toad.

"Mom takes care of me," I said.

"I'm glad you feel that way," Big Bill said, his voice coming out in hard, flaky pieces. "Gives me permission not to."

Big Bill Cuthbertson was a saddlemaker. He didn't call himself that. He would rather say he ran a small store that sold useful things to ranch people. He admitted he could hand-make almost anything a horseman wanted. He was proud of that. But he'd taken himself out of the game of making trophy saddles for the rodeos and for rich people. He had walked away from his halfway-famous reputation. Penny said it was A.J.'s death that did Bill in. A.J. was wild and ornery and just as two-sided as his own father. He could sit for hours and tool a piece of leather. He could also raise hell and indulge his temper and cuss out friends and family with the best of them. But Bill had been certain they would someday go into business together. Then A.J. died.

My mother never said to me that she had a brother. She said her parents hated everything to do with the modern world, that they weren't open-minded enough to deal with her, that Lost Cabin was smaller than a speck of fly shit.

Big Bill continued to ignore me. He liked it when I filled up Mike's water dish. And he liked how I never made noise. But he wasn't one to dole out compliments. He mostly worked in quiet, too. If somebody came into the front part of the building, the tack store, he knew he would eventually hear them. He refused to put a bell on the door. And he told Penny there was no reason for him to waste his time leaning over a counter like he was a jeweler with something symbolic to sell.

"You could be a little friendlier," Penny said.

"Everybody knows what my prices are," Bill said. "Besides, I can see their vehicles when they park. Then I decide if I want to be friendly, or if I don't."

So I was the only one in the tack store when the woman came in with the two children. The woman was tiny with a round, crinkled face and large glasses. Her hair was frizzed into a cap of black curls, and she wore an old-fashioned coat, the kind with square pockets and buttons the size of store-bought cookies. She also carried a stretched-out looking purse. The children were young, maybe three and five. One was a boy with fat cheeks and bright, snowman eyes. His hair grew straight away from his head like he was made of static electricity. The other kid was a girl, or that's what I decided. I couldn't tell. Its hair was long. Its eyes were black. Its hands were wet from where they'd been jammed into its sticky mouth.

Indians. I was from South Dakota. I knew Indians.

The three of them stood in the doorway for quite some time. I knew the woman could see me, even though I was scrunched behind the stool Big Bill left in the corner where he displayed his silver belt buckles. But she didn't say anything, and I didn't say anything. I wasn't sure where Big Bill was. He liked to go back to the house and eat bacon sandwiches whenever he felt hungry.

The littlest kid stayed close to the woman, right against the swing of her heavy coat. The boy not so much. I kept waiting for him to get a move on and start messing with Big Bill's stuff.

It never happened.

The woman did one thing before she left. She leaned toward where Bill hung his curb bits and his snaffle bits on a dusty square of wallboard. She touched one of the bits. It was hard for me to tell, maybe she touched two of them. It looked like she closed her eyes. Then she shuffled herself right around, making sure the children were with her, and left the store without a question or a sound.

"That's Rosie Real Bird," Big Bill said, appearing in that coyote-along-the-fence way he had. "She works in Dr. Van Camp's office. Hell, she works a lot of places. She's trying to decide if she should order a new bridle for her oldest grandson. She likes the designs I can carve into a headstall. Does the beadwork herself—some of the best you'll ever see. She's been in here three times. I hope that grandson knows how much she loves him."

"I wasn't gonna let them steal nothing," I said.

"Don't have to worry about that," Bill said, hitching up the jeans he liked to wear so loose. "Rosie and me understand one another just about perfect. She's got to be with something a while before she can buy it."

I could hear Mike scrabbling to his feet from where he lay on the concrete floor next to Bill's workbench. Mike had just about gotten to the point where he'd let me open a door for him so he could go outside.

"I didn't trust them kids," I said, almost whispering.

"Makes you even, then," Bill said. "Because I guarantee they're suspicious about you. Rosie's gonna wonder what I done to earn myself a prejudiced grandchild after all these years."

I felt the skin around my eyes start to burn.

"God damn, Annette," Bill said, looking up into the crowded rafters of his store. There were wagon wheels up there and boney-looking things I'd come to know were saddle trees. "She always did know how to make me feel mad and pitiful at the same time."

They talked about school. I heard them. Assuming I had the count right, I'd been with them nine days. I hadn't been to school on a regular basis since my mother had it out with the social worker at Roosevelt Elementary. I could read. I could add and subtract. I could scramble eggs with milk and salt. I could beg for change at a laundry mat.

A.J. was killed when his excavator rolled into an irrigation ditch. He was stone-cold sober. He knew how to swim. It didn't matter.

Big Bill called me Missy. He said he didn't understand the extra-long, foreign-sounding name my mother had put on my birth certificate. That name involved more syllables than I needed. "I'm not saying you ain't special," he told me. "But a girl as interesting as you don't need such a big announcement."

He let me watch him work. He showed me his tools—it seemed like there were hundreds of them and most looked like pieces of junk. "First stamps I ever made come from nine-penny nails I stole from Mickelson's Hardware," he said. "That's how the old-time cowboys done it, filing stamps from nails and quarter inch bolts. They lived on the road following ranch work wherever it took them. Evo Parsons paid for his winter room and board with the wallets and belts he carved at night."

"You ever live on the road?" I asked.

Big Bill paused before he answered me. He knew it was a trick question. "Four years in the army," he said. "That's the only hoboing I'm willing to admit to right now. Why don't you and me cut a deal? I'll give you the scraps from that calfskin I'm using to make Ned Shepperson the fancy parade chaps he's too damn old to wear, and you stop quizzing me like a lawyer. Calfskin is from Taliaferro's in Tennessee. Best hide I got in the shop right now." He gave me the cold owl eyes from behind his wiry glasses. "Consider it a bribe."

I practiced in the front of the store where Bill couldn't see me. I felt stupid with the stamps and the mallet. Basketweave. Scrolls. A squashed crown shape Bill had created that he called the Wyoming daisy. I tried all the easy designs. But I felt stupid. And unsatisfied. And pissed off. I swung the mallet until my fingers bruised. The marks I left in the leather looked like chewings from a rat's teeth. Still, I kept going. I wanted to tool that hide into *my* shape, just right. Bill had told me he'd teach me how to two-tone leather with his tiny, tiny brushes. He said he thought I had the steady hands for that.

I was pounding so hard on my little calfskin map of the universe I didn't hear the man come into the store. He was like most of Bill's customers—slow-moving, tip-toey when they were closed into a space smaller than a barn. I don't know how many times he cleared his throat before I heard him.

"Bill here?" he asked.

Bill wasn't in the shop or the house, either one. He'd gone to Riverton without saying why. Penny had asked me to call her on the intercom if we got a customer. I shook my head.

The man was younger than I'd thought at first, seventeen or eighteen, with a face as staring and creamy as my own. He'd taken his hat off before he asked his question. Spikes of hay spilled from the hat brim to the floor. His blond hair was spiraled from sweat. I could see a pair of work gloves flapping from the back pocket of his jeans.

"I come to pay for my rope," the man said. "I reckon I can leave the money with you, if that's all right."

I felt a familiar ripple run from my armpits into the circling of my ribs. I nodded to the man. "Sure."

The man pulled a buck-stitched wallet from his other back pocket and counted out one-hundred-and-twenty dollars in cash. The wallet was hand-carved with a wild rose design. I knew enough to recognize that now. I wondered if Bill had made it. "Testerman," the man said, wiping his damp forehead before he reset his hat. "Will Testerman. And tell Mr.

Cuthbertson I'm grateful he's willing to stretch me a good rope. His are the best." The man coughed his way through an embarrassed smile before he left. I let the money lie on the counter next to my humiliated calfskin until the good feeling had drained out of each and every green bill. Then I took it.

It felt like a thick, black electric cord plugged into my belly, the need to get back to my mother. The feeling hadn't been there so much at first. Annette wasn't shy about taking breaks from me. She talked about it, and she did it. I had decided it was all right if I took a break from her. Plus, Penny was nice. She wasn't the kind of woman who kept score or changed her mind from one second to the next. But the electric cord was there, inside me, connecting. I hadn't told Big Bill the whole truth. Yeah, my mother took care of me. I also took care of her. I was the one who made sure we had blankets wherever we were staying. I was the one who made sure there was something to eat at dinner time, crackers at the very least. My mother liked hot soup and crackers.

I could hitch a ride back to Rapid City. I just needed to avoid the cops.

Big Bill and Penny didn't lock up anything except the tack store. I took a black shoulder bag that Penny used to carry checks to the bank, and I took the cheese and cold sausage from the refrigerator. Penny had bought me a blue fleece pullover. I took that, and two sweatshirts, and I stole Penny's silver-threaded blouse because I knew it would look good on Annette. It was just the right size. One hundred and twenty dollars. I kicked Mike's water bowl over right after I stole two of Bill's best knives from his work bench. I left the water to spread out over the floor, like a puddle of piss.

It was a frosty night in Wyoming. I didn't mind. The state highway was so close I could see beams from the cars swinging like flashlights through the dark.

The man who picked me up didn't look all that nice. He was driving a company truck, one of those white dually GMCs that the oil and gas outfits buy. My mother had taught me about company trucks. They were as safe as the U.S. Postal Service, she said. Just tell them it was a fight with a boyfriend. Or bad treatment from a stepdad. But don't ever get into a man's private vehicle, she told me. That was a top-of-the-list rule. I wasn't old enough to make that gamble. Neither was she.

The man, who smelled like a sack full of Egg McMuffins, was sneakier than he looked. He said he was on his way to Casper. He turned down his radio and offered me a cigarette. It was a Salem. He lit it for me.

"My grandpa's been beating on me," I said. "It's bad. I can show the bruises."

"It takes all kinds," the man said, looking at me with uneven eyes. "I'm glad to get you off that cold road." He had the style of hairy, unshaved neck me and my mother hated, but he made sure I got no kind of feeling from him, even though he didn't know I had Bill's sharp knives in my pockets, one on each side. Which is why I believed him when he slowed down in Riverton and said he needed to stop for coffee. The sheriff's office. He delivered me right to the door.

Penny, when she was done flapping her hands and thanking the deputies, said it was time she and Bill told me the truth, what little they knew of it. My mother had been in jail, yes. But she was out, she had been out for four or five days, and she had called them. They had also heard from a lawyer, though some of what the lawyer said was confusing. Annette wanted me to stay in Lost Cabin, she'd been clear about that. She might have to disappear for a while. It was that or testify.

"You're lying," I said to Penny. "Me and my mom have a rule. We don't let ourselves get separated by other people. Ever."

"I don't know what to say, hon," Penny said, her face starting to twist in a way I hadn't seen before.

"She wouldn't do this to me," I screeched.

"Sure she would," Big Bill screeched back. "Let's get that through your thick skull. You think this is the first time we ever laid eyes on you, that we didn't keep you here when you was a little bitty thing? You been out in the wind before, girly. If you believe Annette's finally got the goddamn world by the tail, go right ahead and steal you a sack of things and get gone. But I won't have you calling your granny a liar."

"Bill—." Penny tried to interrupt. The boniness in her shoulders looked sharp enough to break.

"I know what you're gonna say, Penny. You gonna say I'm too hard on this one like I was with her mother. But I can't...I can't let another child from this...I feel like with this one we need to say just how bad the whole thing has got."

There was silence in the kitchen. Big Bill was breathing so hard it sounded like he was drawing air right out of his skinny legs.

"What Bill's saying," Penny whispered as she wiped some tears off her lips, "is your mom begged us to come get you in Rapid City. Begged us. We hadn't heard from her in...years. I...she didn't even know about... about our A.J." Penny couldn't go on. It was hard for me to listen to her, anyway. My ears felt like they were melting into nubs of wax. Why hadn't Annette talked to me on the phone? Why hadn't my mother called for me?

"She knew there was gonna be a raid," Bill said, looking up into the air like he did when he wasn't ready to take the world on eye-to-eye. "She knows the boss hombres will be coming for her."

My mother liked to fight with waitresses. They were too slow, she said. Too poor. They smelled of stale ketchup and didn't care how they looked. "Don't you dare turn into somebody who stops working on her style," she told me. "It's best to keep citizens guessing, especially the men ones. Anytime the world don't feel big enough, you just remind yourself you got the sweet moves to make it bigger."

Big Bill knew I'd come. I couldn't sleep. He couldn't sleep. I slipped into his workshop wearing the pink-spotted pajamas Penny had bought for me. They stunk of plastic wrap. They were the first real pajamas I'd ever owned.

"There's some prime craftsmen who can dye or stamp when they are drunk," Bill said. "I ain't one of them. I've had some beers, that's a fact. And here I am, wishing for coffee, weaving on a martingale ordered by some sour-voiced gal who lives up in Jackson Hole. What do you have to say, Missy? You here to steal more of my knives?"

I shook my head.

"I believe you owe me a hundred-and-twenty dollars. Should I put you to work?" he asked. The lenses of his glasses looked like white shields blocking out his eyes.

"We got to help my mom," I said.

"No, we don't," he said.

"But she…." I couldn't finish my sentence. My heart and lungs began to punch at one another, hard, and before I knew it I was crying, something so forbidden it wasn't even on the list of rules.

"Oh, little miss," Bill said, sighing, "we are in a bad way here." He bunched his shoulders together like he wanted to stand up from his workbench and maybe even come closer to me, but he didn't do it. "You are making me feel older than spit."

"Annette can't do jail," I said, tasting my own punk salts in my mouth. "Everybody knows that."

Bill pulled his glasses off and rubbed the skin on the sides of his nose like that skin was dirty. "It's the damnedest thing," he said. "Neither one of my kids ever come crying to me out here. They was both water spouts, don't get me wrong. And your mother could bring on Noah's flood when she wanted. But she didn't try it out here. Penny says it's because they was afraid of me."

"I ain't afraid."

"No, Missy, you ain't. And that's part of the problem. You see that saddle over there?" Bill asked, knuckling one of his hands in the direction of the racks that hung on the workshop wall.

I saw a lot of saddles. Bill had as much repair business as he wanted.

"That one there," he pointed, "under the gray cover. It's the saddle A.J. was working on when he got hisself killed. It's a good design, maybe even a great design. He had the gift. He thought he could sell that saddle for nine or ten thousand dollars, and he was probably right. He'd ordered the custom silverwork. It come in the mail after the funeral, and I thank heaven Penny never saw the postman that day. It would have broke her in half. A.J. started with a tree made by Gilberto Ruiz over in California, and he did everything meticulous after that. I almost didn't recognize him when he was carving the fenders. He was like a different body with different eyes in his head."

"Annette goes crazy in jail," I repeated.

"You said that already. I'll get to Annette. Right now I'm telling you about my son. *My only son.*"

I shut my trap. Big Bill was swinging his voice at me like it was a snow shovel.

"I'll be sorry to my death that you've had to live in a world where people don't behave decent and kind," he said. "I don't know what else Penny and me could've done. I made plenty of mistakes in my life, most of them with Penny, most when I was younger. I know what it feels like to have demons in your belly. I pretty much got on my knees the last time I saw Annette, and she wouldn't even let me see your face. I went to another lawyer in Riverton last week. You didn't know that, did you? Unfortunately, he don't have any brilliant ideas. He says I could go to South Dakota and talk to the government people there."

"Take me with you," I said, feeling my chest fill up with bat wings.

"I've thought about it," he said. "But I doubt we should be telegraphing the fact Annette has a pretty little girl."

I closed my eyes, trying to keep the leakage in. My mother had this thing she did with her long fingernails, drawing pictures on my back when I was feeling sick or sad. Cats with whiskers. Rattlesnakes.

"I want you to walk over there and take the cover off that saddle," Big Bill said. "I do it at least once a year. It cooks my guts every time."

I stood still, wishing I could feel the blood in my feet, which I could not.

"Go on," Bill said.

"Why?" The word was like a fish hook in my mouth.

"Because I said so, damn it. Because you've become a irritating obligation in my life, and I want to know whether you're more like your mother or more like my poor dead son. None of us will ever figure out who your daddy was, so we'll get no satisfaction there."

He came up beside me then, Bill did, and he shoved me halfway across the workshop floor. I could feel his hot beer breath blowing across my eyes. He tore the cover off the saddle and threw it somewhere. He took my right hand and smashed it down onto the saddle's cold, quilted seat.

"Feel of that," he said, crushing my fingers under his. "It's not *ever* gonna get finished. It's a beautiful thing. A honest thing. And my boy wasn't give the chance to finish it. The way I was brung into the world, if a man don't finish a thing in his life, it lays after him in ruins no matter what kind of ribbon you try to tie around it later. Your mother has burned every ticket she ever got. She don't care about nobody but herself. I want you to think about that. What it means. You can't protect her, Missy, even if you want to. I can't protect her, either, not from the hawk that's on the wing this time."

"You don't love her," I said, squirming. "You don't even care."

Big Bill leaned what felt like all of his weight onto my hand. My finger bones started to burp out of their sockets. "Is that what you think?" he hollered. "If that's what you're saying after all this time in my house, then I just got a answer to my goddamn question."

They came on motorcycles. Penny was at a meeting of the Jacob's Daughters. Then she was scheduled to drop by Kettle Creek School to see what it would take to get me enrolled. I was in front, in the tack store, too mad at Big Bill to tool on any leather and too mad to stay by myself in the house, either one. I used the store phone to dial my mother's cell number, the one she'd had for the last three months. It was something I'd already tried more than a hundred times. Still no answer. None. All I got was the purring way she said "Honeys, leave a message." Then it happened. Bill was able to see the bikers from his bench in the workshop before I even had a clue.

He came through the connecting door in a foxy sideways motion. "Little Miss," he said, his voice more formal than I'd ever heard it. "I need you to take Mike and go out the back right now."

I wouldn't even look at him. I pretended I was memorizing the horse magazine I had on the counter in front of me. I tried to work more spit into my mouth so I could give him some hell when I had the chance.

"You need to hear me, girly. Take the dog and leave. Run. Don't stop at the house. Get to Lone Eagles' Garage if you can do it without being seen. Tell George I asked you to call 9-1-1."

"Wh—?"

"Your mother's friends," he said. And that was the end of it.

I wish I could say I ran to my grandpa's side and hugged him like he deserved. I wish I could say I barricaded myself—with Big Bill—in the workshop, both of us bristling sharp with awls and knives. But me and Bill didn't have any rules, except for maybe the one I didn't want to admit to: That it's all right to love a person even if you don't trust them. I looked at Mike, who'd turned into a gray bullet of fur, and asked him to come with me. He did it, even though the sounds of heavy biker boots were already thumping at the tack store door.

"To George," Bill said, his breath huffing a little in his broad-banded chest. "So nobody can see you."

It takes longer for a person—even a tough girl, even a desperate one— to cover necessary ground than you might think. I sailed. And Mike sailed with me, staying just off my heels with his yellowy teeth bared like he knew what dog protection meant. I felt pure and fast, but I wasn't. Later, I'd find out it had taken me more than three minutes. Then I had to spit out my story to George Lone Eagle and his brother, Knot. Then they had to believe me. Then they had to make the phone call. Lost Cabin is smaller than a speck of fly shit. It keeps one policeman on duty at a time, especially on good weather afternoons.

Later, I'd find out Big Bill played it steady and hard. He tried to talk them out of it. He told them Annette wasn't in the shop or the house. He said he'd sent her to Canada. With her little girl. They could beat on him, Annette's father, if they wanted. They could try to kill him or burn him out, but his answers weren't going to change. They had no business bringing their fists and chains into a man's place of business, anyhow. That was the cowards' way.

They tried it—to kill him and burn him out. Then they rode their farting bikes back out of town.

Later, Penny would tell me Bill had been in fights when he was in the army that caused problems with his intestines. This fight made those problems worse. My grandpa, Big Bill Cuthbertson, who has a saddle on display down in the state museum that I someday hope to see, didn't die right away. We saw him. We talked to him in the Riverton hospital, and I spent a little time sitting by his white bed holding onto his big veiny fingers. But he couldn't talk back to us, not very well. So I had to tell him the things I thought he should know. I had to tell him in my best voice.

How he was no kind of ruin and how I wasn't going to be one, either.

How he'd taught me to always finish a thing, even if I couldn't finish it in a happy way.

How we can, all of us, step in front of another person's failure and take the crushing blow. It's not a rule, that kind of step. It's more an unplanned flight of the heart.

Author Biographies

Susan Austin grew up mucking in Chesapeake mud, but the western mountains captured her affection. She lives in the foothills of the Tetons. She was a Michener Fellow at University of Texas. Her work has appeared or is forthcoming in *BOAAT, Clerestory, Borderlands, Hanging Loose, and Open Window.* Words abandoned her for a time, but they return spirited, full of the wildness she loves in this country.

Betsy Bernfeld is a librarian and lawyer in Jackson Hole, Wyoming. She is a recipient of the Wyoming Arts Council's Frank Nelson Doubleday Award for a Woman Writer. Her anthology of historical Wyoming poetry, *Sagebrush Classics: Pure Wyoming Stuph,* was published by Media Publishing, Kansas City, MO. Her own poems have recently appeared in *Black Hills Literary Journal, Manifest West,* and *Labyrinth,* a WyoPoets chapbook.

Autumn Bernhardt writes, teaches, and speaks about the land, water, and cultural resources of the West. She is a Colorado native and is of mixed Lakota descent. She has been a Tribal Attorney, a clerk for a judge, and has represented Colorado in U.S. Supreme Court litigation involving interstate rivers. Autumn currently teaches Indian Law, Natural Resources Law, civil rights, and persuasive writing.

Constance Brewer's poetry has appeared or is upcoming in *Harpur Palate, Tipton Poetry Journal, Dark Matter Literary Journal, The Linnet's Wings, The Nassau Review,* and in the *New Poets of the American West* anthology. Constance holds an MFA from the University of Buffalo and is co-editor for *Gyroscope Review.* She is a recipient of a 2016 Wyoming Arts Council Fellowship grant, and lives in Northeast Wyoming with a small but vocal herd of Welsh Corgis.

Birgit Fowler Burke, born in the flat Midwest, is derived from silent, self-sufficient farmers and storytelling immigrant Swedes. Musician, writer, and artist, she says her creativity isn't so much a vocation as a lifestyle. She writes to commemorate people and places, with sad words about suicides, bitter ones about bad lovers, sweet ones on hope, and musings on weather. She moved to Wyoming when she was young and has been here ever since. She loves Wyoming.

Lynn G. Carlson lives on the prairie east of Cheyenne with a retired firefighter and a span-triever. She has published in various literary magazines and has an essay in National Public Radio's *This I Believe* archives. Lynn blogs at writingwyoming.com and recently edited the anthology *Watch My Rising*. Her Wyoming roots go deep, and there's no place she'd rather be, except sometimes in February.

Carolyn Grant Castano lives in Centennial with her husband, Francis. She is a graduate of the University of Pennsylvania and a former member of the Pennsylvania Council for the Humanities. Her love of books began as a child. She has two adult children, Susanne Foy and Matt Castano.

Su Child uses writing as her way of capturing new perceptions. Sculpting with words, she shares exceptional moments. At the website Mentation—meditativewriting.com, Su encourages others to do the same. In learning to retire as an Indian Education Resource, she enjoys curating the annual Cody City Hall exhibit of Contemprary Native Heritage.

Celeste Colgan lives near Centennial, Wyoming. She has been a teacher, college professor, business administrator, think tank fellow, and has worked for state and federal government. Now, she identifies herself as a full-time fiction writer. She is working on a collection of Wyoming short stories.

Edith Cook. Before immigrating to the U.S., Edith worked as industrial translator in German/English and German/French. She raised her family in California, where she worked in her late husband's law office. She has taught in two-year colleges and at universities in South Dakota and Tennessee. On retiring she moved to Cheyenne, and later removed to her farmland. Edith's columns appear weekly in the Wyoming Tribune Eagle and the Casper Star Tribune. Find more at her website, www.edithcook.com.

Julianne Couch is a prose writer and native of the Midwest, but after almost 20 years in Laramie, considers herself a Wyoming writer. In 2011 she relocated to Iowa. Now she writes about Wyoming, Iowa, and the places in between in the region. Her latest book, *The Small Town Midwest: Resilience and Hope in the Twenty-First Century*, was published in 2016 by the University of Iowa Press.

Matt Daly's poetry has been published various journals including *The Cortland Review, Pilgrimage, Sixfold, Clerestory*, and *Split Rock Review*. He was the recipient of the 2015 Neltje Blanchan Award, and in 2013, he received a creative writing fellowship from the Wyoming Arts Council. From his home base in Jackson,

Wyoming, Matt teaches high school English and is faculty member of the Jackson Hole Writers Conference.

Susan Davis is a Laramie, Wyoming photographer. She focuses on the shifting, surprising light as it plays across the vast expanse of the high plains and mountains of Wyoming. Her images can be viewed online at susandavisgallery.com, and in Laramie, at the Works of Wyoming gallery.

Jason Deiss was born in a small desert town where he continues to spend time in the surrounding landscape. He enjoys most games, and spends time trying to make art out of sound, food, and words.

Maureen Dempsey is a recently retired English and Social Studies High School teacher who has relocated to Pinedale, Wyoming from northeastern Nevada. She graduated from the University of Wyoming and began her teaching career on the Wind River Indian Reservation. Her poetry has been published in Great Basin College's literary magazine, *Argentum*. She is happy to be back in Wyoming.

Carol L. Deering grew up in Western Mass., but has lived in Wyoming for 30+ years. She has twice received the Wyoming Arts Council Poetry Fellowship. Her poetry appears most recently in *Written River* and in *Soundings Review*. She also has poems in the anthology *Ring of Fire: Writers of the Yellowstone Region*. Once she had the privilege of interviewing Richard Hugo; that interview, published by *Art Notes* (Columbia Basin College), was reissued in *CutBank*.

Tammy Dominguez writes because she must! Getting published is a bonus. Tammy has a Bachelor's degree in English from the University of Wyoming. She writes mostly poetry and short stories. She is passionate about nature, animals, creating art, writing, reading, cooking and she dreams of traveling the world. She dreams of publishing her own book of poetry and a book of short stories. She is a copywriter and lives in Casper with her granddaughter, Aliyah, and five Chihuahuas.

Jane Dominick recently moved back to Cody, Wyoming, after living in Laramie where she took writing courses at the University. She has been an English teacher, a program director at the Humanities Council, and co-manager of a dude ranch. She has a horse and a dog. Her prose and poetry celebrate life and the natural world.

Maria Lisa Eastman always suspected that horses were her next-of-kin, and they've been her guides. From the back of a horse, she got curious about native grasses and earned a master's degree in watershed management. These days she ranches with her husband in northwestern Wyoming and runs a non-profit horsemanship program, Rainhorse. She'll be performing at the National Cowboy Poetry Gathering in Elko, Nevada, in 2017. Her love for the Western landscape inspires her poetry.

Diane Egge and her husband have lived in Cheyenne, Wyoming, for the past twenty-five years. She enjoys riding her horse in the mountains. Besides poetry, she also endeavors to capture the beauty and uniqueness of Wyoming with her photography. She's previously been published in *High Plains Register* and *Weather Watch, Poems of Wyoming*.

Art Elser retired after 20 years as an Air Force pilot and 30 as a technical writer. He has a PhD in English and taught writing for over 30 years. His poetry been published in *Voicings from the High Country, Owen Wister Review, High Plains Register, Science Poetry, The Avocet*, and many others. His chapbook, *We Leave the Safety of the Sea*, received the Colorado Authors' League Poetry award for 2014.

Deborah Schmitt Emmerich has lived in Wyoming for the last 35 years. She and her husband currently reside in Cheyenne. Deborah holds a BS from both South Dakota State University and the University of Wyoming and a MS from Montana State University. As a retired educator, enjoys finally having time to pursue her interest in writing. Deborah draws inspiration from her experiences as a rural school teacher and from spending time with her husband in the wilderness.

Shanna Ferguson has spent most of her life living in and adapting to the extremes that are Wyoming, which inform her poetry, essays, and short stories. She is a member of WyoPoets, Wyoming Writers and Prairie Pens Writer's Group in Gillette. Recently, two of her poems were published in the Wyoming Writer's 2016 Chapbook, "Labyrinth". She and her husband, Ken, live on a small rural acreage outside of Gillette, Wyoming with her beloved horses, his farm-size garden, and their "labradorable," Jed.

Patricia Frolander and her husband, Robert, own his family ranch in the Black Hills of Wyoming. Her first book, *Grassland Genealogy*, was published in 2009 followed by her second, *Married Into It*, which garnered the National Cowboy and Western Heritage Museum's coveted Wrangler Award for Best Poetry Book of 2011. She won the Willa Cather Award for Best Poetry Book, as well as Best Woman Writer by High Plains Book Awards, 2012. Frolander was appointed Wyoming Poet Laureate in 2011.

Gene Gagliano. Wyoming's new Poet Laureate, Eugene M. Gagliano, is best known for his collection, *Prairie Parcels,* and his children's poetry book, *My Teacher Dances on the Desk* (winner of the 2010 Delaware Diamonds Book List Children's Choice Award). Gene is a retired elementary teacher, and author of *C is for Cowboy* and the award winning *Dee and the Mammoth.* Gene's poetry has been published in many magazines and anthologies. He lives with his wife Carol near the Big Horn Mountains.

Sunnie Gaylord is a former co-editor for *Open Window Review* and a current student at the University of Wyoming. She is a fifth generation Wyomingite. She spends her free time drinking bad wine with good friends.

Corinna German writes creative non-fiction with the beautiful Absaroka-Beartooth Wilderness of Wyoming and Montana over her shoulder. As a life-long hunter and naturalist, she offers readers an antidote to the frantic pace of urban life through her nature writing. Corinna is a member of Wyoming Writers, Inc. and Scribophile. When she's not dodging grizzlies or stalking elk, you can find her in Laurel, Montana with her husband and four boys.

Vickie Goodwin is a passionate Wyoming native, and a graduate of Casper College and the University of Wyoming. Her varied career paths have included waitressing, teaching, selling Tupperware and working as a community organizer. Vickie has traveled widely, but Wyoming always pulls her back where she belongs. Since retiring in 2004, she enjoys writing both fiction and nonfiction.

Teresa Griswold is a writer and designer based in Jackson, Wyoming. A conservationist who relishes the wild, open, natural spaces of the valley she calls home, she is dedicated to preserving the environment through her writing. When she is not writing, editing, and designing for various publications, she devotes her time to poetry. Her collection of poems entitled *Twelve Poems of Christmas* was released in a limited edition in 2013.

Alyson Hagy is the author of seven works of fiction, including the novel, *Boleto*, and the story collection, *Ghosts of Wyoming*. She lives in Laramie, Wyoming.

Jeanne Shaw Hauf grew up in Salt Lake City and Seattle. She came to Wyoming in 1993 on a summer lark. Twenty-one years of marriage, two teens, and loads of nature and wildlife experiences later, she writes non-fiction and poetry with occasional forays into novel-writing. Jeanne is online at windblownword.blogspot.com

Marcia Hensley studied at the University of Tulsa, and for many years lived in Farson, Wyoming, with her late husband, Mike. Now retired from the faculty of Western Wyoming Community College and living in the Denver area, Wyoming remains the inspiration for her writing. She is a member of Wyoming Writers.

Rose Hill. Born on a farm near Cainsville, Missouri, in 1931, Alta Rose Hill came to Wyoming with her mother and three sisters in 1947. She and her husband adopted three children. Now widowed, Rose is grandmother six times over and great-grandmother to five. Governor Mead appointed her to serve as Wyoming's seventh Poet Laureate from July 2015, to July 2016. She is a member of two state writers' groups and two local groups in Sheridan—Range Writers and Third Thursday Poets.

Aaron E. Holst spent many years in public service as a firefighter and fire chief in Wyoming and Montana. His poetry and prose have appeared in *Wyoming Voices, Chaparral Poetry Forum, Distant Horizons, Sandcutters, Off Channel, Encore, Emerging Voices, Voices Along the River, Labyrinth*, and numerous other journals.

Lori Howe is the author of *Cloudshade: Poems of the High Plains*, and *Voices at Twilight: A Poet's Guide to Wyoming Ghost Towns*. She has taught English and creative writing for a decade, and is currently a doctoral candidate in Literacy Studies at the University of Wyoming. She lives in Laramie, Wyoming, and is the editor for *Blood, Water, Wind, and Stone: An Anthology of Wyoming Writers*.

Michele Irwin has made her home in Wyoming since 1987, though she has lived in the same sage steppe region most of her life. She has a Master's of Public Administration from the University of Wyoming, is a board member of the Wyoming Outdoor Council, and a longtime member of both the Wyoming Wildlife Federation and Wyoming Writer's Inc. She and her husband live with their Airedales and a small herd of bison along the Green River in Sweetwater County.

Cindy Jackelen lives in Buffalo where she is a Literacy Facilitator for the Johnson County schools. A former newspaper editor, she has written much of her life. She is currently working on a memoir. Recently she and her young grandson co-authored their first song. In 1996 she and her students discovered hundreds of deformed frogs, launching an international scientific investigation.

Cornelius F. Kelly is an octogenarian (January 16, 1936) who has found fulfillment through the writing of poetry. It has allowed him to view the world around him through a magnifying glass. It has directed his focus, clarified his thought, and shaped his language. It makes the ordinary special. It gives beauty to the common. It elevates the soul.

Echo Klaproth is a 4th generation Wyoming rancher. Her writing reflects the legacy of: family, life's struggles, gains and growth as a daughter of Christ, as well as the blessings of being born and raised in Wyoming among good and honest folks. She retired from teaching, was ordained a minister, and serves as Chaplain with a non-profit hospice organization. She and her husband live on a small farm near Shoshoni.

Earle Layser. Author of six books and numerous magazine and anthology stories, Earle F. Layser writes from Alta, Wyoming. His most recent book is a true love story set within the Greater Yellowstone—Teton region, *Darkness Follows Light: A Memoir of Love, Place, and Bereavement*, available at bookstores and Amazon.com.

Stephen S. Lottridge is a former professor of Slavic Languages and Literatures and a psychologist. He is a native westerner and has lived in Wyoming—Rock Springs, then Jackson--for the last twenty-eight years. He currently focuses on writing essays, poetry and plays, and is an actor. He is the father of three grown, adopted children. He is especially concerned with the environmental impact of our species on the rest of the natural world.

Beverly Leys is a Wyoming writer who uses writing to sieve—and save—those moments and experiences that mark our interactions as both sacred and humbly human. She is currently off the grid in the Canadian wilderness with her family, living and writing where no phone or politics can reach her.

Susan Vittitow Mark is a publications specialist at the Wyoming State Library in Cheyenne. She began as a reporter in Utah, going on to own and publish the *Tongue River News*, edit *The Sheridan Press*, and write for the *Wyoming Library Roundup* magazine. Her poetry appears in *High Plains Register, Tulip Tree Review*, and *The MacGuffin*. Susan is the WyoPoets webmaster, a past president of Wyoming Writers, and one of the two writers behind the Writing Wyoming blog at www.writingwyoming.com.

Susan Marsh lives in Jackson, Wyoming. With degrees in geology and landscape architecture and a lifelong interest in creative writing, her work explores the relationship of humans to the wild. Her work has appeared in journals that include *Orion, North American Review*, and *Fourth Genre*, and in many anthologies. Her books include the award-winning novel *War Creek, A Hunger for High Country*, and *Cache Creek: A Trailside Guide to Jackson Hole's Backyard Wilderness*.

Renee Meador is a retired secondary mathematics teacher who lives in Big Horn, Wyoming. A member of Range Writers, Third Thursday Poets, Wyoming Poets, and Wyoming Writers Inc, her writing has been published in several anthologies and journals as well as online at www. cowboypoetry.com. Renee enjoys being outdoors, preferably on a horse. Renee has two grown children, Charles Meador and Amelia Heizer, and seven grandchildren.

Erik Molvar is a wildlife biologist. He has worked as a professional conservationist to protect Wyoming's wildlife and public lands for 16 years. His 16 guidebooks to national parks and wilderness areas include guidebooks to Glacier, Olympic, and Zion national parks, and a backpacking techniques manual for Arctic regions. He writes as a political pundit in the DC-based journal *The Hill*, and has contributed social commentary in Laramie's *News from Nowhere*. He lives in Laramie.

Carrie Naughton is a freelance bookkeeper who writes speculative fiction, environmental essays, and poetry. She has moved away from and back to Jackson, Wyoming five times now since 1996. Her work can be read at *Strange Horizons, Zoomorphic, Star*Line*, and *The Tishman Review*. Find her at carrienaughton.com. She blogs about whatever captures her interest.

Shelly Norris. Born in The Garden City of Wyoming, Shelly Norris considered Yellowstone her back yard. As a Winter Soul, Norris suffers interminable ophidiophobia. She is a committed cat person and animal lover and daily practices tolerating the human race as a group, though she is a people person one-on-one. She now resides in Missouri with her White Knight and their pet menagerie. Mucho Gusto!

Bret Norwood is a poet, storywriter, and conlanger from Sheridan, Wyoming. As a writer, he admires the honesty of the modernists, the nobility of the classics, and the imagery of the fantastic. Find links to published stories and poems at bretnorwood.com.

Brian Nystrom lives and works in Jackson, Wyoming. He is a contractor, a bicyclist, and an Episcopal priest. His poetry has been published in Clerestory: Poems of the Mountain West.

Lyndi O'Laughlin has a degree in nursing, and has studied poetry under the guidance of Boston poet Matthew Lippman for the past three years. She reads and writes from her home in Kaycee, Wyoming, where she lives with her husband, John, two dogs, and a few chickens.

Myra L. Peak received an Independent Artist Grant from the Wyoming Arts Council in 2010, a WAC poetry fellowship in 2007, and recipient of the WAC's 2004 Frank Nelson Doubleday Award. Her work appears in journals such as *Owen Wister Review* and *High Plains Register*, and has won awards from Wyoming Writers, Range Writers, WyoPoets, and Western Wyoming College. Myra's writing reflects an emphasis on the High Desert and oil, gas, and mining. Myra is the current president of WyoPoets.

Jordan Rich lives in Jackson, WY, where she works at the Teton County Library. She has previously been published in *Feast Magazine, Cruising World Magazine* and anthologized in the *Capable Cruiser* by Lin & Larry Pardey.

Mike Riley grew up in Forsyth, Montana and has an MFA from the University of Montana. After 40 years of teaching, he retired in 2014 and became a mentor for the Journalism Education Association, which recently honored him with their Lifetime Achievement Award. He has won the TransAtlantic/ Henfield Award for short fiction and Wyoming and Montana literary fellowships. He is currently working on a memoir and is teaching again at Cody High School.

Jay Robbins was born in the 1980s. He grew up in Wyoming. His writing generally mimics dog shit sprinkled with glitter, though he infrequently pursues other forms of the written word.

David Romtvedt was born in Portland, Oregon and received an MFA in poetry from the Iowa Writers' Workshop. He has worked as a carpenter, bookstore clerk, letter carrier, college professor, blueberry picker, musician, and ranch hand. His most recent book is Zelestina Urza in Outer Space, a novel published by the University of Nevada Center for Basque Studies in 2015. His next book of poems, Dilemmas of the Angels, will be published in Spring 2017 by Louisiana State University Press. A recipient of two NEA fellowships, the Pushcart Prize, and the Wyoming Governor's Arts Award, Romtvedt served from 2003 to 2011 as the poet laureate of Wyoming.

Linda Ruhle has published and won awards for her poetry, essays and short stories, and has written five books. Raised in Northern California, Linda migrated to Ten Sleep, WY, in 1996. She loves learning, nature (rocks, bones and feathers), people, travel (Paris!), and Sunrise and Bella, her two cats. Deliriously retired, she roams between Wyoming and California, and is a full-time optimist and writer.

C.C. Russell lives in Casper, Wyoming with his wife and daughter. His writing has recently appeared in such places as *Tahoma Literary Review, Word Riot, Rattle,* and *The Colorado Review*. His short fiction has been nominated for a Pushcart Prize, Best Small Fictions, and Best of the Net. He has held jobs in a wide range of vocations—everything from graveyard shift convenience store clerk to retail management with stops along the way as dive bar dj. He can be found on Twitter @c_c_russell

Tim Sandlin is a novelist and screenwriter. His novels include *Sex and Sunsets, Western Swing, Honey Don't, Jimi Hendrix Turns Eighty,* including his newest novel, *Lydia*. Movie credits include the Showtime original *Floating Away,* based on *Sorrow Floats,* and *Skipped Parts,* a TriMark film. He is also a contributor to the New York Times Book Review and has judged several writing competitions, including the Western States Book Awards. He is director of the Jackson Hole Writers Conference.

Dawn Senior-Trask grew up in a log cabin in the Snowy Range foothills. Her father was an author and artist, her mother adept at homemaking under rough conditions—no electricity or plumbing—and her older sister and brother were both published poets. Since age six her writings, drawings and woodcuts have appeared in anthologies and books. She is also a bronze sculptor. She lives with her husband and family—including six horses and a donkey—near Encampment.

Michael Shay's book of short stories, *The Weight of a Body*, was published by Ghost Road Press in 2006. His fiction and essays have appeared in journals such as Flash Fiction Review, Silver Birch Press, Northern Lights, and High Plains Literary Review, and in numerous anthologies, including *In Short, a Norton anthology of brief creative nonfiction*. Michael lives in Cheyenne and blogs at hummingbirdminds.

Patti Sherlock lives in a 1902 farmhouse and walks her dogs on foothills east of her home or in the river bottoms to the west. She writes and raises bees. Sherlock has published three nonfiction books and three youth novels, plus numerous magazine pieces. Her book, Letters from Wolfie, won two literary prizes in Japan, the Merial Human-Animal Bond award, and was chosen as a "One City-One Book" selection by cities in Colorado and California. She is resident faculty for the Jackson Writer's Conference.

Barbara M. Smith has published in *The Last Best Place, Wyoming Fence Lines, Deep West, A Literary Tour of Wyoming, Leaning into the Wind, Woven on the Wind,* and *Crazy Woman Creek,* and many other collections. She received the Neltje Blanchan award for nature writing in 2008, the Wyoming Governor's Arts Award in 2006, the Wyoming Arts Council Literary Fellowship in 1990, and a residency at Ucross. Smith taught English and creative writing at WWCC in Rock Springs, WY, retiring in 2008. She lives in Rock Springs, Wyoming.

Melissa Snider is an elementary school librarian and writer who has lived in Wyoming for more than 25 years. She has bachelor's degrees in Creative Writing and Spanish from the University of Montana, and a master's degree in Library and Information Science from Simmons College in Boston. She grew up partly on the shore of Lake Ontario in upstate New York, and partly in the shadow of the Tetons in Jackson Hole.

Tom Spence was born in Sheridan, Wyoming in 1940 and graduated Laramie High School in 1958. He received a Bachelor's in Art and English in 1963 and an MA in Art in 1964, both from the University of Wyoming. His career has included teaching college in North Carolina, Connecticut, New Jersey, and New York City; working underground for the NYC Transit Authority; and small business owner—he built and ran Tom's Main St. Diner in Buffalo, Wyoming before retiring—again—in 2006. Tom serves on the board of Wyo Writers, Inc., is a father and grandfather, and is married to Vikki Chennette who, as of this writing, is still putting up with him.

Jennifer Stewart Fueston lives and writes in Longmont, Colorado. Her poems appear in *The Priscilla Papers, Relief,* and *Ruminate,* and are forthcoming in *The Cresset* and *Windhover.* Her first chapbook of poetry, *Visitations,* was released by Finishing Line Press in 2015. Jennifer holds degrees in rhetoric, composition and literature. She has taught writing at the University of Colorado, Boulder, as well as internationally in Hungary, Turkey, and Lithuania.

Kim Strellis and her family were led from the Midwest to the Tetons of Wyoming in the 1980s. Inspired and guided by her creator, she is working on a spiritual memoir titled, *Assigned Seat.* Her poem, "Standing in the Creek", appeared in the 2015 JHWC special issue of *Clerestory: Poems of the Mountain West.*

Tory Taylor. In 1971, Tory Taylor left Colorado, saddled his riding horse, tied a diamond hitch on a pack horse, and headed north. A few weeks later he rode into Dubois, Wyoming, where he met his life's partner, Meredith, and the two were married in 1978. Tory and Meredith learned the outfitting trade by working as wranglers, packers, guides, and cooks; in 1980 they started their own Northwest Wyoming backcountry outfitting business and have recently retired.

Chris Valentine. Born in England, Christine Valentine lived in Montana for fifty years and recently moved to Sheridan, WY. Christine writes poetry and non-fiction. She worked for the Northern Cheyenne Tribe until she retired. Her work is included in many publications including, *Emerald Coast Review; High Plains Register; The Avocet Nature Journal; Lowdown Literary and Arts Journal* and *Big Sky Journal.* She was nominated for a Pushcart Prize in 2015.

Lindsay Wilson is an English professor in Reno, Nevada where he co-edits *The Meadow*. He has published five chapbooks, and his first book, *No Elegies*, won the Quercus Review Press Spring Book Award. His poems have appeared in many journals including The Missouri Review, Verse Daily, and The Bellevue Literary Review. He serves on the Nevada Writers' Hall of Fame Selection Committee.

Connie Wieneke has lived in Wyoming since 1983. In 1991 she earned an MFA in creative writing from the University of Montana. Her poetry has appeared in print and on line in Stand, Owen Wister Review, Whiskey Island Magazine, Cutbank, Descant, Silver Birch Press, and Clerestory Poetry Journal. A piece is forthcoming in The Artists Field Guide to Greater Yellowstone (ed., Katie C. Holsinger, Torrey House). One of her day jobs is as assistant director for the Jackson Hole Writers Conference.

Sue Wilcox lives on North Piney Creek in Story WY. She writes, edits and translates technical and research work. She studied prose and poetry in UCLA Extension classes. She depends on StoryTellers, Sheridan's 3rd Thursday Poets and author Diane Lefer for critique and guidance. Sue serves on the Story Community Library Board.

Vicki Windle is a poet, an artist, and a singer/songwriter in Casper, Wyoming. A member of Casper Writer's Group and of WyoPoets, she has read and performed at Nicolaysen Art Museum, various coffee houses in Casper, and Patris Art Studio in Sacramento, CA. She is illustrator and publisher of a series of mini poetry books: "From My Hands to Yours 2016," and is published in 2014 WyoPoets publication, "Weather Watch: Poems of Wyoming."

Caridad Woltz has been a Spanish teacher by day and a writer by night for many years. She enjoys writing poetry in English and in her native Spanish, with themes that frequently broach issues of loss and healing. A graduate of the University of Utah with a Master's degree in Languages and Literature, she could be found writing in the hidden library nooks of the towns of Salt Lake City and Jackson.

ENJOY OTHER SASTRUGI PRESS TITLES

Cloudshade by Lori Howe

In every season, life on America's high plains is at once harsh and beautiful, liberating and isolated, welcoming and unforgiving. The poems of *Cloudshade* take us through those seasons, illuminating the intersections between the landscapes surrounding us and those inside us. Extraordinarily relatable, the poems of *Cloudshade* swing wide a door to life in the West, both for lovers of poetry and for those who don't normally read poems. Available in print and audiobook formats.

Voices at Twilight by Lori Howe

In Voices at Twilight is a collection of poems, historical essays, and photographs that offers the reader a visual tour of twelve past and present Wyoming ghost towns. Contained within are travel directions, GPS coordinates, and tips for intrepid readers who wish to experience these unique towns and town sites for themselves.

Cache Creek by Susan Marsh

Five minutes from the hubbub of Jackson's town square, Cache Creek offers the chance to immerse ourselves in wild nature. *Cache Creek* shares some of the ways you can do it. No experience needed: bring your attention and a few hours of your time. You will be enchanted. Cache Creek is a popular hiking, biking and cross-country ski area on the outskirts of Jackson, Wyoming, drawing several dozen to several hundred people per day. Use this unique guide to find your way.

Antarctic Tears by Aaron Linsdau

What would make someone give up a high-paying career to ski across Antarctica alone? This inspirational true story will make readers both cheer and cry. Fighting skin-freezing temperatures, infections, and emotional breakdown, Aaron Linsdau exposes harsh realities of the world's largest wilderness. Discover what drives someone to the brink of destruction while pursing a dream. Available in print and audiobook formats.

The Blind Man's Story by J.W. Linsdau

Imagine one's surprise to be hiking in the great Northwest and coming across someone who is blind and spends his summers living high on a mountain. That's what happened to journalist Beau Larson. He returns to work to cover a dispute between local timber workers and environmentalists. Beau finishes his report, but soon discovers there is more to the story than he thought.

Journeys to the Edge by Randall Peeters, PhD.

Ever wonder what it's like to climb Mount Everest? The idea isn't as far-fetched as it may seem, even though very few people in the world have climbed Mount Everest. It requires dreaming big and creating a personal vision to climb the mountains in your life. Randall Peeters shares his guidelines to create a personal vision.

Roaming the Wild by Grover Ratliff

Jackson Hole is home to some of the most iconic landscapes in North America. In this land of harsh winters and short summers, wildlife survive and thrive. People from all around the world travel here to savor both the rare vistas of the high Rockies and have the chance to observe bear, moose and elk. It is an environment like no other, covered in snow most of the year yet blanketed by wildflowers for a few precious months. This place is both powerful and delicate.

Prevailing Westerlies by Ed Lavino

The clarity of Ed Lavino's images conveys an intensity of feeling that commands attention. His photographs speak of a longing to be part of the natural world while questioning and challenging our destructiveness. Lavino's mastery of the black and white image equals that of the best 20th century photographers, yet his work is decidedly modern. His unconventional intellect and perspective will transfix and delight.

Visit Sastrugi Press on the web at www.sastrugipress.com to purchase the above titles in bulk directly from the publisher. They are also available from your local bookstore or online retailers in print, ebook, or audiobook form.

Thank you for choosing Sastrugi Press.
"Turn the Page Loose"

www.sastrugipress.com

CPSIA information can be obtained
at www.ICGtesting.com
Printed in the USA
FSOW01n0337261116
27726FS

9 781944 986032